We Count On You...!

Please Help Us...?

Myth: Snakes found in India can spit venom.

Fact: No Snake found in India can spit venom. Only Spitting-Cobras can spit venom and they are not found in India.

Myth: There are "Two-headed" snakes.

Fact: The Snake-charmers spread the myth about the Two-headed Snakes only to maintain the mythological status of the snakes in India so they can continue attracting large crowds to their Snake shows. In reality nothing like a Two-headed Snake exists.

Myth: If one Snake is killed its partner will trace you (no matter wherever you are).

Fact: Snakes are not vengeful animals and are not interested in chasing or tracing people who hurt them. They do not have the necessary memory and intellect to remember people to trace them back. Neither do snakes have a feeling of camaraderie nor do snakes pair for life. Once again Bollywood is responsible for this myth.

Myth: Flying Snakes can pierce somebody's forehead or put out their eyes.

Fact: A Flying Snake does not actually fly but only glides through the air by extending its ribs and pulling in the underside. It can glide a distance of 330 feet or 100 metre. It has an elongated head, which gives the scary feeling that it can pierce a person's head or eyes.

Myths & Facts About Snakes...

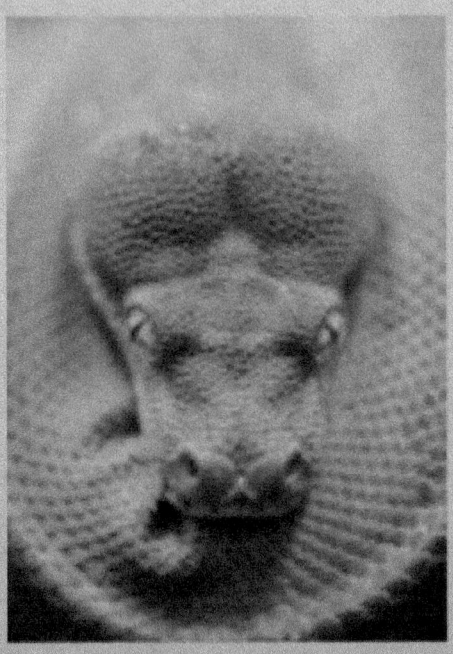

Myth: Snakes remember you if you hurt them.

Fact: Snakes are not vengeful animals and do not have the necessary intelligence to remember people or places for getting revenge. Hindi Movies (Bollywood) have a lot to do with the creation of this myth.

Myth: If one Snake is killed its partner will trace you (no matter wherever you are).

Myth: Snakes drink Milk.
Fact: Snakes drink water and do not drink milk; neither can they digest it properly. They are reptiles and have no association with milk, only mammals that have mammary glands can produce milk and thus a liking for milk in non-mammals is unlikely. But in a crises when severely dehydrated, a snake might drink any liquid available.

Myth: Some Snakes grow a beard as they get older.
Fact: Snakes are reptiles and do not have any hair on their bodies let alone a beard. It is impossible for them to have beards for their bodies do not have any ability of growing hair.

Myth: Snakes carry a diamond in their forehead.
Fact: It is impossible for a Snake to carry anything in its head. The mythological status attached with a Snake in India is probably responsible for this myth.

Myths & Facts About Snakes...

Myth: Rat Snakes are poisonous.

Fact: Rat snakes are Non-poisonous, rodent-eating Reptiles.

Myth: Rat Snakes mate with cobras.

Fact: Rat Snakes or any other snakes will not mate with any snake out of its own species. Cobras eat other snakes so a mating between a Cobra and a Rat snake is not possible.

Most Intriguing Facts About Snakes...

Snakes are covered in scales.

Snakeskin is smooth and dry.

Snakes shed their skin a number of times a year in a process that usually lasts a few days.

Some species of snake, such as cobras and black mambas, use venom to hunt and kill their prey. Read more venomous snake facts.

Snakes smell with their tongue.

Pythons kill their prey by tightly wrapping around it and suffocating it in a process called constriction.

Some sea snakes can breathe partially through their skin, allowing for longer dives underwater.

Anacondas are large, non-venomous snakes found in South America that can reach over 5 m (16 ft.) in length.

Most Intriguing Facts About Snakes ...

Snakes are carnivores (meat eaters).

Snakes don't have eyelids.

Snakes can't bite food so have to swallow it whole.

Snakes have flexible jaws which allow them to eat prey bigger than their head!

Snakes are found on every continent of the world except Antarctica.

Snakes have internal ears but not external ones.

Snakes used in snake charming performances respond to movement, not sound.

There are around 3000 different species of snake.

Snakes have a unique anatomy which allows them to swallow and digest large prey.

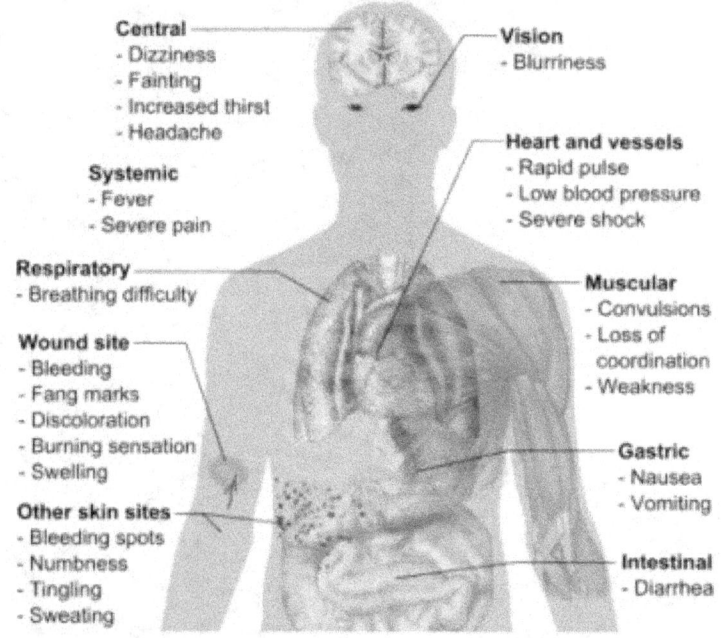

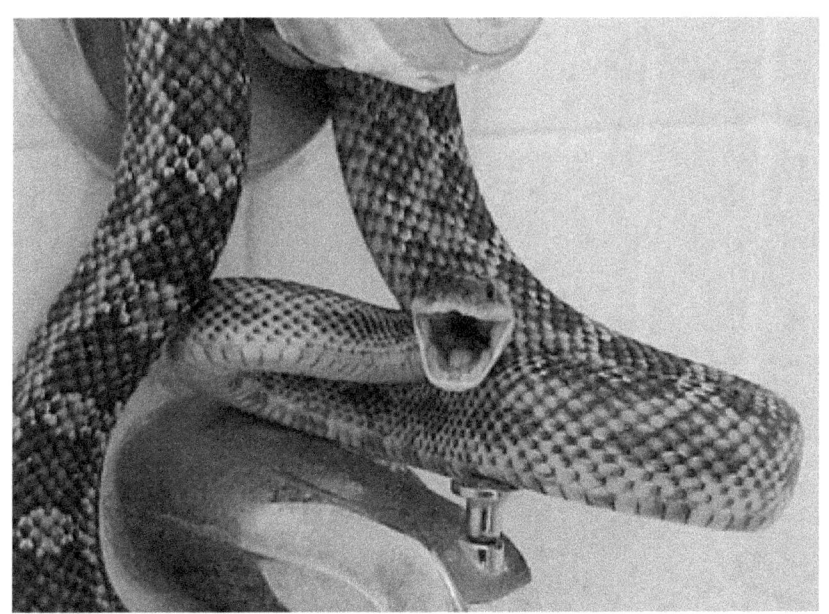

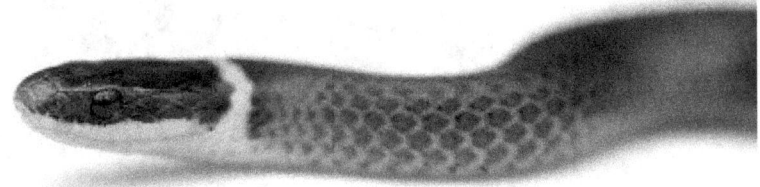

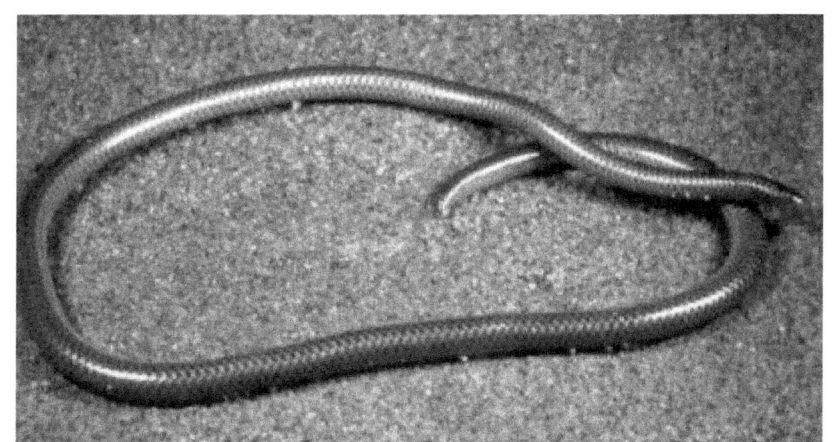

...To Cute Baby Snakes...

To Hatching Snakes...

Mother Instincts...

Snakes Mating...

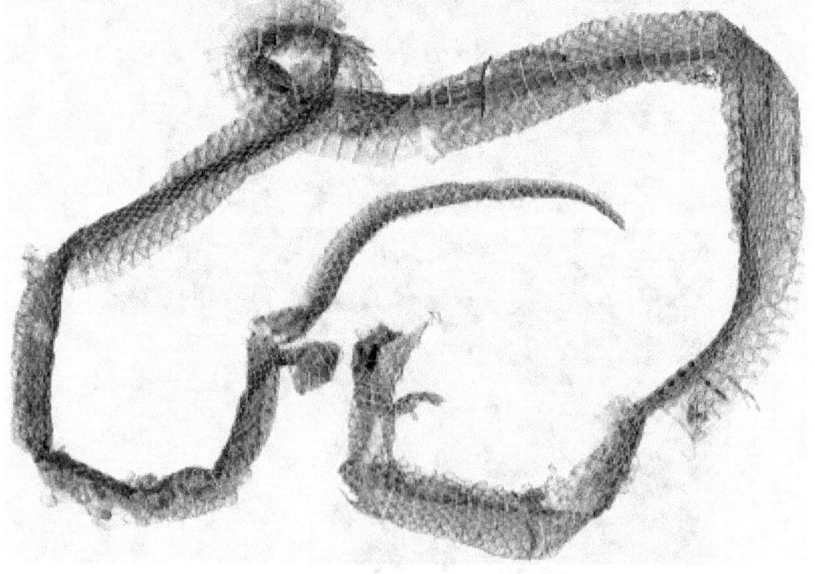

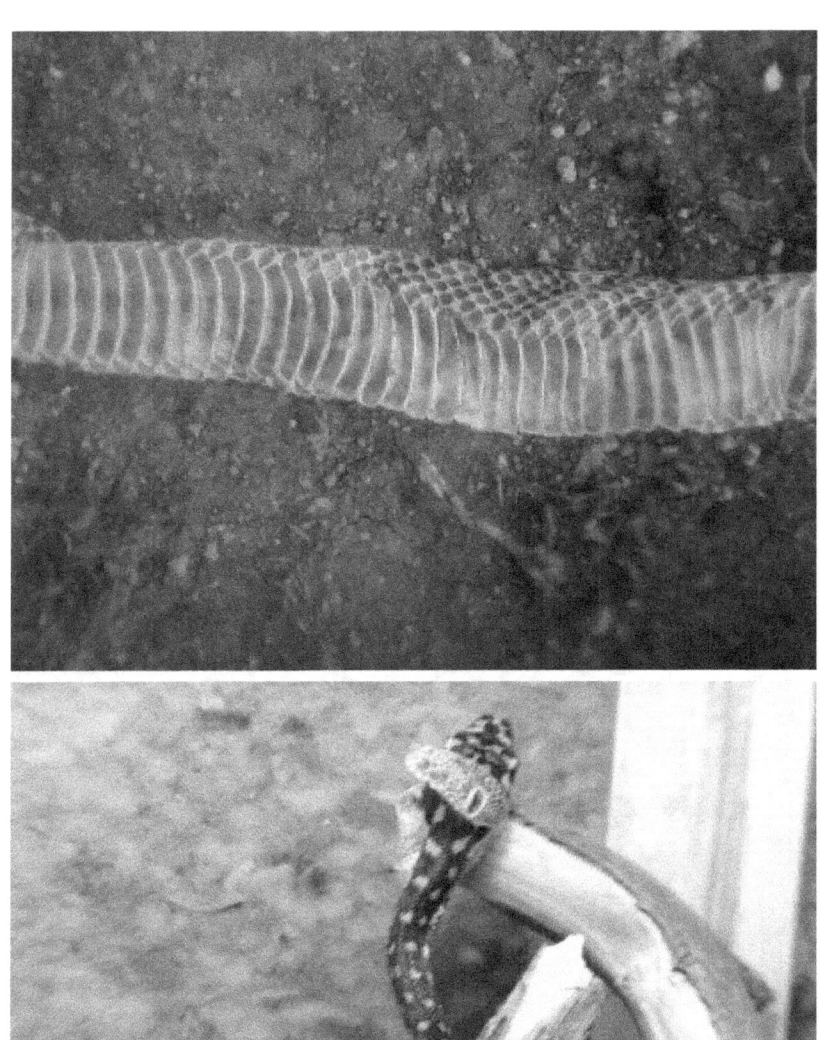

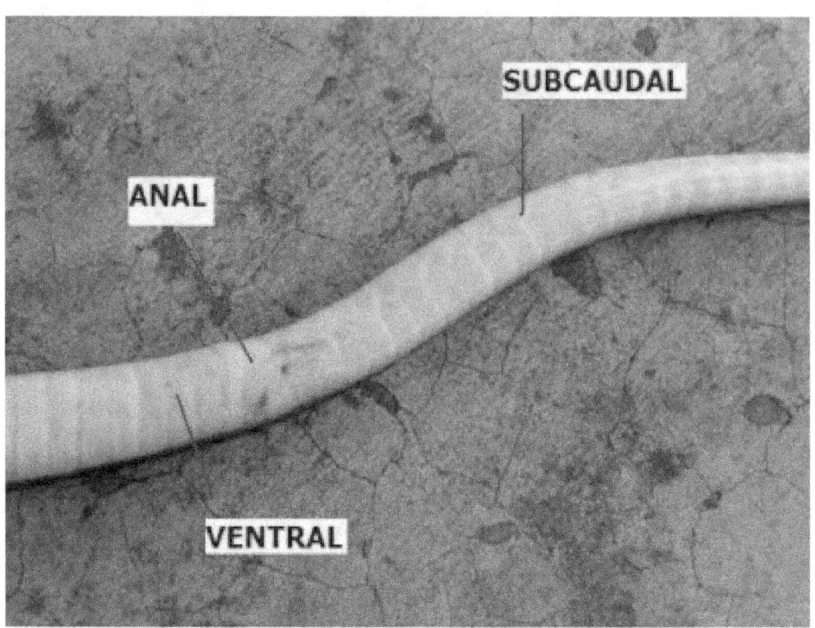
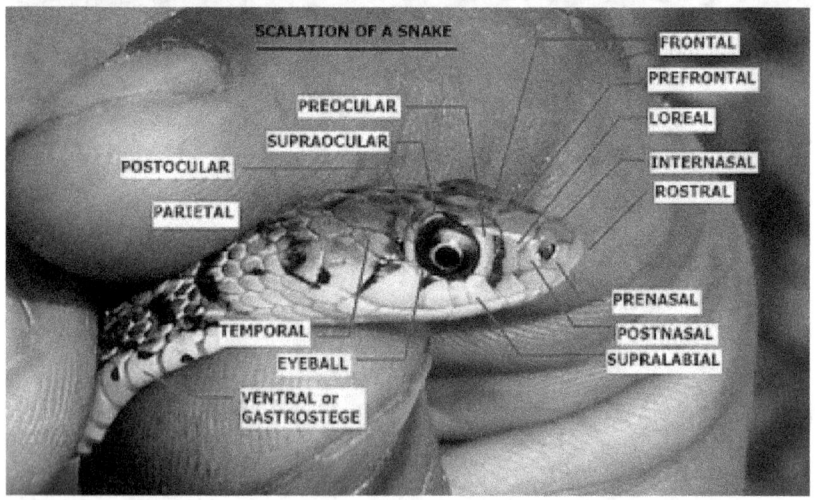

1. Esophagus
2. Trachea
3. Tracheal lungs
4. Rudimentary left lung
5. Right lung
6. Heart
7. Liver
8. Stomach
9. Air sac
10. Gallbladder
11. Pancreas
12. Spleen
13. Intestine
14. Testicles
15. Kidneys

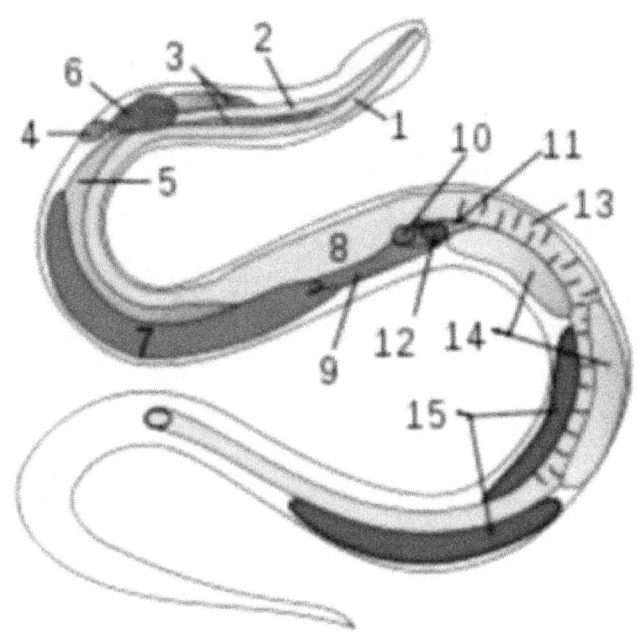

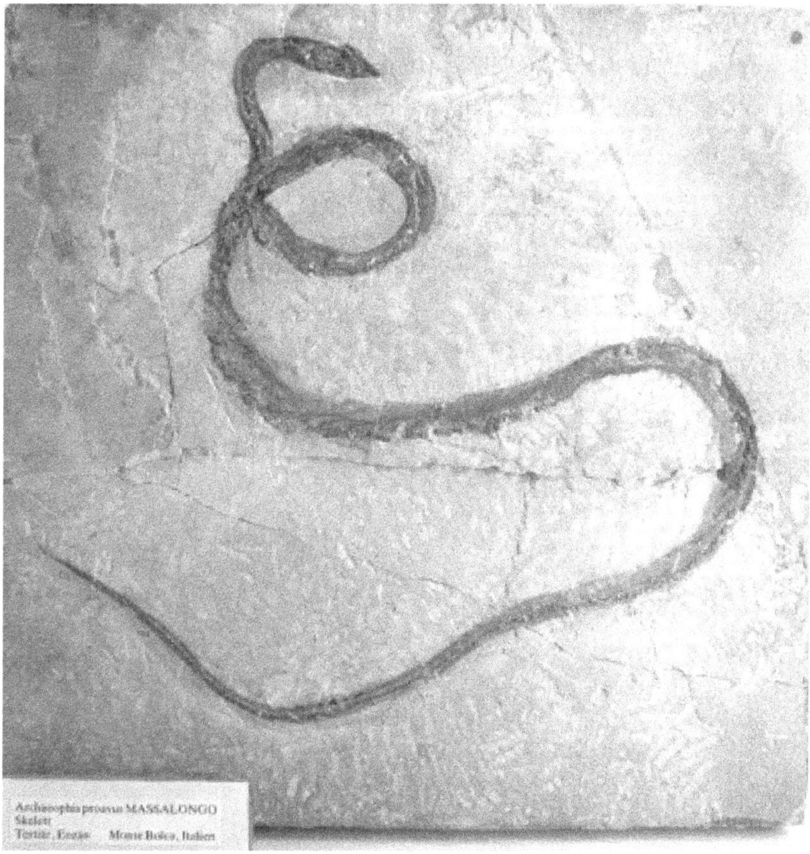
Archaeophis proavus MASSALONGO
Skelett
Tertiär, Eozän Monte Bolca, Italien

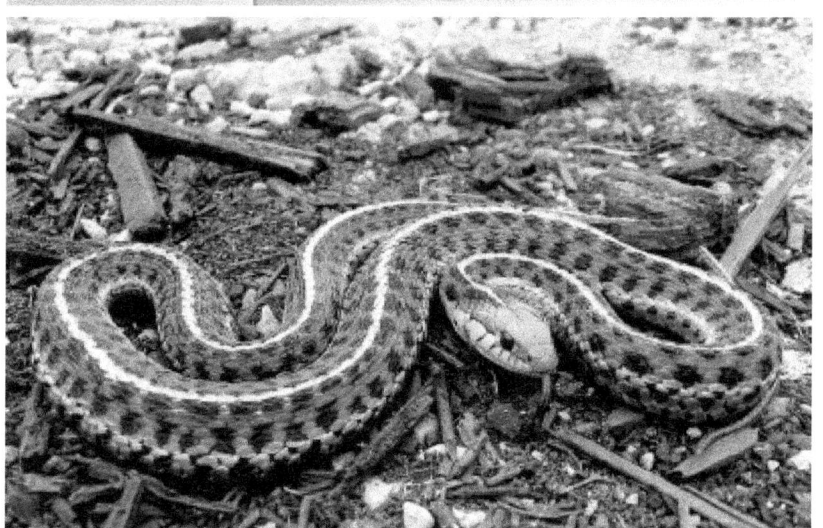

While every precaution has been taken in the preparation of this book, the publisher assumes no responsibility for errors or omissions, or for damages resulting from the use of the information contained herein.

SNAKE DISCOVERY KIDS: JUNGLE STORIES OF MYSTERIOUS & DANGEROUS SNAKES WITH FUNNY PICTURES, PHOTOS & MEMES OF SNAKES FOR CHILDREN

First edition. July 26, 2017.

Copyright © 2017 Kate Cruso.

ISBN: 978-1386306177

Written by Kate Cruso.

My Favorite Quote

Source: Steve Jurvetson
"The snake which cannot cast its skin has to die.
As well the minds which are prevented from
changing their opinions; they cease
to be mind."—Friedrich Nietzsche

Introduction

The reason why I wrote this snake discover book as part of my "Discover Book Series" is an important one.

Every child should know about the issues that relate to snakes because snakes are cool, calculating, beautiful, reckless animals that first have to be understood before they can be judged. Snakes are also wise and intelligent and we as humans can learn an awful lot of these mysterious creatures.

Snakes are part of the reptile world and should never be confused with amphibians (frogs, for example, are amphibians).

By the way, did you know that snakes have a 6th sense?

You will find out more of these fascinating snake facts and curious snake stories in the chapter that talks about some amazing snake revelations, myths and truths & other curious stuff about snakes and in this chapter you will find out the ultimate answers about all your snake questions.

Once your kid has gone through this discovery book, he or she will agree that snakes are truly amazing!

The fact that snakes are approximately 90 million years old (other experts say that snakes are even up to 155 million years old) and were able to survive through evolution until today truly makes them reptile stars!

It is true the snake is one of the most ancient species on the globe, but sadly enough some of the snake species are declining and some rare species are even considered endangered today.

In a concerted effort we must all be aware of the decline of some of the snake species and help to save them!

This book will provide your child with all the facts, stories, and pictures that are related to the world of snakes. Having a better understanding of who the snakes really are, from where they come, and how they relates to us humans is key to a better understanding of the world of animals and nature in general.

It is important for your child to understand how snakes help balance the ecosystem that humans, plants, and animals live in.

Once your child does understand all these relationships, he or she will be able to have a better appreciation for snakes and animals in general.

Your child will also discover many interesting, curious, and intriguing facts about snakes which will in turn help your child appreciate a snake's existence.

After having read the book your child will be better able to understand why snakes are so precious to us humans and why we need to save their heritage.

By reading the book your child will personally get in touch with some amazing snake moments and this alone is worth going through the discovery phase that this book is going to provide your child with.

In the end your child will know more cool things about snakes and this knowledge will enrich your child on a mental level because knowledge is power.

If your child is an informed kid, he or she knows more stuff which in turn will enable him or her to get into a deeper discovery process and this in turn will help raise your child's interest level making him or her more involved and engaged in life in general.

This active mental discovery process will ultimately lead to a higher intelligence level.

Once your child is knowledgeable about the species of snakes, he or she can decide which way to go from here and he or she can truly start a positive mental relationship and friendship with this beautiful and mysterious animal.

Who knows but maybe this information is going to be the basis for some of your kid's future initiatives. Based on information like this your child might engage his or her initiative for the cause of snakes or any other endangered animals at a later point in time.

Helping shape a positive future and helping shape the intelligence of responsible individuals who are going to care for extinct animals and who might one day bring their own resourcefulness, responsibility, and initiative to the table is part of the reason why I made it my mission to create this discovery series.

This snake discovery book is the fifth volume within this discovery book series.

As a mother of twin boys and a little girl, I know that I want to be actively involved in their educational process to help shape their visions, imaginations, dreams, hopes, creativity, and their positive involvement with everything that this beautiful world of ours has to offer.

I have set my goal to help kids envision and discover intriguing, amazing, and curious stuff that they find cool and that is part of our life here on earth.

Encouraging them to view life from a totally new perspective and dimension helps kids build new mental connections between things that they might not have considered before is what I want to achieve with my books that I am writing for children about animals, nature, space, and other related issues.

Going through such an active discovery process helps stimulate the active thinking and contemplation process which in turn increases a child's intelligence in general.

Involving your child with a positive, creative, mentally involving and stimulating, interactive, and responsive educational discovery process where your kid gets satisfactory answers back is how you help shape the intelligence of your child.

If you are letting your child explore new and cool things about a subject, you are making an active contribution into your child's future! Such an investment into your child's future is the most valuable investment that you can ever provide your child with.

This book will empower your child to raise and get answers for questions like why some snake species are endagnered, why the snake is such an amazing animal, why it is important to save the snake, what your child can do to help the endangered snake species, and lots more.

These are just some more additional reasons why this snake discovery book provides such an important contribution into your child's educational process and mental development.

Once your child is aware about all these issues that surround the snake, he or she will feel more enriched and in tune with the nature, the world of the animals, our environment, and our earth.

Helping to protect the valuable species that have been brought to us by mother nature is one of our priorities as human beings.

We as human beings can create a healthy balance and we as human beings have the intelligence to create a balanced, protected, happy and peaceful life between humans and animals happen.

As you can see there are many reasons why reading this frog discovery book is an important step into the future of your child.

I wrote the book in the most positive spirit and my main goal for the book can be summarized as follows.

As a mother it is my responsibility to entertain and engage my kids with positive educational content. In my opinion as a former first grade teacher,

mother nature provides the richest sources of valuable content for a child. Human beings, animals, and plants are a good way to get your child started with the discovery process.

My kids always tell me that they love to be entertained while they discover something new at the same time. Learning about some cool new information is how they learn best and they love to consume a mixture of pictures, funny facts, stories, and the curious and intriguing side of a specific animal or topic that they are learning about.

I know from my own experience as an educator and researcher and from my interaction with children in general that kids love to learn stuff the cool way.

I listened to kids and took the responses that I got from them and it is my goal to surprise them with a real cool book series. This discovery book series

is basically inspired by kids. It is made from kids for kids. It respects the way kids like to learn.

I created this book series in a way that respects the way how kids like to learn because they told me what they find cool and groovy and I listened to them and included it.

The book contains lots of pictures, cool facts, and other curious and intriguing stuff that kids just seem to be fascinated with.

This specific discovery book is about snakes and therefore it fulfills a second big goal. This book can also be seen as a contribution to help endangered snakes and to help stimulate children to contemplate about the endangered species of snakes.

This book should raise awareness about this endangered species in the eyes of a child. It should help a child be aware that it is possible between humans to sustainably coexist with snakes.

Lastly, I want to stress that this book is there to enrich your child's spirit, imagination, creativity, hope, dreams, and vision about the wonderful world of snakes.

A child must know that he or she has a stake in such a global cause like snakes.

Reading about today's issues in such a positive and mentally stimulating way helps empower a kid's creativity, initiative, and interaction to create a better and happier future for a life in balance with the nature.

A child should also know that although the situation of the snakes is very delicate, there are positive news in regards to the recovery process of declining rare snake species because there are human beings who act in a very responsible way that snakes to sustain themselves in the nature by extending the nature reserves and by developing new projects and snake breeding and snake protection programs in a concerted effort to sustainably co-exist and live in balance together with this rare and endangered species of snakes!

I truly hope that you and your child are going to enjoy the concept and the content of this book and I hope you get lots of valuable moments out of this discovery series.

I welcome every parent and child to discover the wonderful world of snakes - one of the oldest and most ancient species on earth, but sadly enough a declining and endangered species at the same time!

Ancient Snake Origins

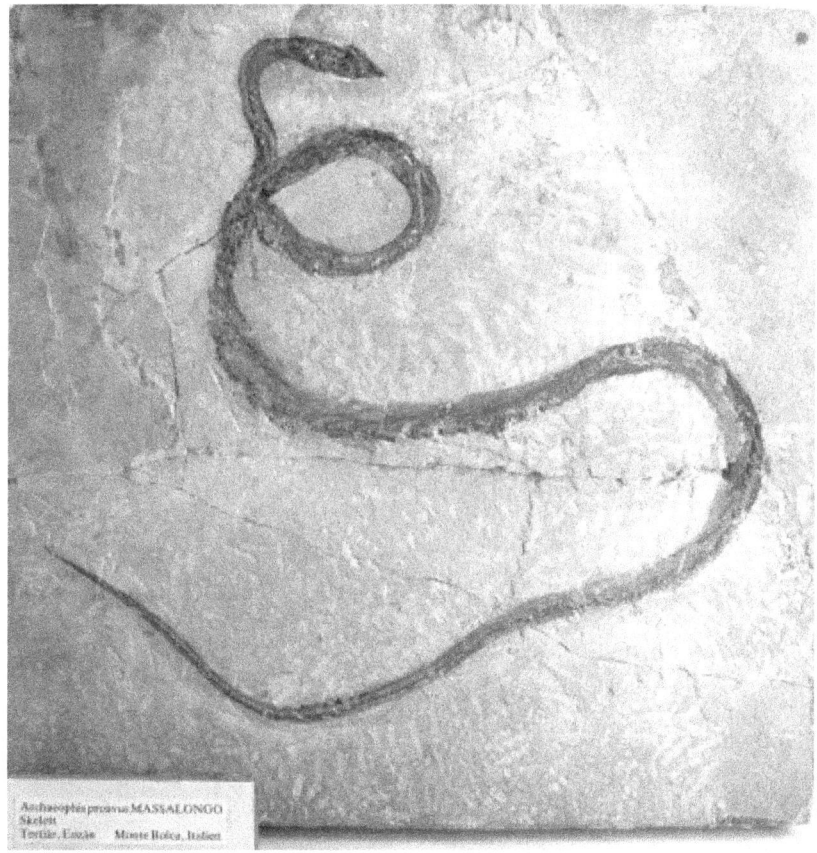

Source: Raymond - Raimond Spekking—Fossil of a Archaeophis proavus Massalongo, Monte Bolca. Museum für Naturkunde (Berlin)

Did you know that we snakes used to have legs?
    It is said that a process of slow and gradual lengthening our body (we originally had a body similar to a lizard) and the loss of our limbs took place during evolution which resulted in snakes.
    Scientists have analysed many fossil serpents of us snakes with legs which give a view that we snakes have originally evolved from sea-living lizards.

This 95 million year old creature was found encrusted in sedimentary rock near Jerusalem.

This period is called the Cretaceous period and it seems to be a very pivotal time in the evolution of snakes and snake history shaping, too. Many snake experts believe that snakes first appeared much earlier on the earth and during the upper Jurassic period (around 155 - 135 million years ago).

INTRIGUING FACT ABOUT SNAKES: DID YOU KNOW THIS CURIOUS FACT ABOUT SNAKE CHARMERS?

Snake Charmer in Jaipur, India

The practice of snake charming is traditionally most common in India. Historically snake charmers have been developed though other Asian nations. These countries include Bangladesh, Pakistan, Thailand, Sri Lanka, and Malaysia.

Ancient Egypt was tradtionally the home to a certain type of snake charmers. From there it spread to India and throughout the North African continent and countries like Morocco, Egypt and Tunisia are well known for snake charmers. Today, however, the art of snake charming is becoming less and less popular because India recently banned the ownership of snakes.

You can still find some snake charmers today and it has not entirely become a lost profession, but as governments are trying to interdict snake ownership, snake charmers who solely depend on this skill which is their only means of livelihood are fighting back in order to keep their rights to own a snake.

Snake Charmer In India

Scientist's results have shown that our snake DNA is significantly different from the DNA of varanid lizards. Our DNA is more like the DNA of other land-based lizards.

They concluded that this is a strong evidence for the existance of a land-lizard, the origin of us snakes.

However, whilst it is agreed that snakes evolved from lizards, the question that paleontologists are now asking is whether these "lizards" were terrestrial, aquatic, or burrowing?

There are many questions answered while there are still many secrets and questions unanswered about snakes, their history and their evolution.

Let's get into the wonderful world of this mysterious creatrue and look at what we humans already know about their secrets.

GLOSSARY:

What are sedimentary rocks?

Sedimentary rocks are specific rocks that are formed by the deposition of rock material at the surface of the earth.

What is DNA?

DNA is a molecule (within every living being) that encodes the genetic instructions for a living being (humans, animals, plants) used in the development and functioning of all known living organisms and many viruses, too.

Snakes Around The World

Human beings have been fascinated and terrified by us beautiful snakes. From the dawn of time and since humans and snakes have been living on earth, humans have loved us for characteristics like virility and good fortune. On the other hand we have been discriminated to be creatures of nightmares and evil. Through the history and evolution of time, we snakes have been misunderstood and misinterpreted by human beings.

We have been associated with occult type of stuff and we have been symbolised evil.

Humans have even been obsessed with our evil side by scaring and terrifying themselves and in a very unreasonable reason via the means of both non-fictional and fictional movies and books about the evils of us snakes.

Source: Marek Szczepanek—Grass Snake

Through knowledge and understanding, passion and empathy for us snakes, you will be able to get a better appreciation of us snakes, our beauty, and our complexities.

We know that humans are looking at us sometimes with disgust and other times with irrational fear of danger and disaster.

As the snake eperts and people who know a little bit more about us snakes, we snakes are not aggressive.

However, if you are walking around in the nature with bare feet after dark and without light and accidentally step on one of us snakes, what do you expect to happen next?

If your answer is the following you are absolutely right. Yes, we snakes have a right to live here on earth, too, and if we feel or get attacked (unintentionally or intentionally) we are defending ourselves just like a human being would do.

Instead of generalizing us and saying that snakes are evil and dangerous, why not change the perspective?

Rather look at us as diverse and evolutionary marvels. You will see that if you transform your prejudices and fears into discovery and knowledge you will be much better prepared for your future here on our beautiful earth.

Replace your irrational fear the danger that you feel when you are thinking about us snakes with an interest to discover one of the most fascinating

creatures of the world: the world of snakes!

If you are looking at snakes from a different angle you will see that you are going to discover a world that changes for your.

If you allow a different lookout and perspective, your sense of interest for us snakes will develop into a sense of acceptance and respect and appreciation for us wonderful animals.

You will see that we can snakes can even teach you so many wonderful things about our own species, the human being.

With these encouraging words let's get into the discovery phase of the wonderful world of snakes, shall we?

Let's first look on the question what are the various snakes around the world to get a more global view of us snakes.

Did you know that we snakes are found on every continent except Antarctica. We snakes do inhabit a wide variety of habitats from mountain ranges, deserts, rain-forests, savannah, forests, and even our oceans, rivers, and streams.

INTRIGUING FACT ABOUT SNAKES: DID YOU KNOW THIS CURIOUS FACT ABOUT US SNAKES?

The largest snake species of us snakes that ever lived on Earth was the "Titanoboa". This boa lived somewhere around 58 to 60 million years ago. The Titanoboa Cerrejonensis species is estimated to have reached the length of 40 - 50 feet and a weight of approximatey 2000 - 2500 pounds. It is believed by humans that the warm climate during that period of time favored this snake species to reach such an enormous size. This giant snake species came into existance shortly after the End-Cretaceous extinction period. The extinction of the large dinosaur species might have caused the arrival of this huge ancestor of us snakes.

Source: L. Shyamal, Wynaad 2006
—Elaborately shaped scales on the
head of a Vine Snake

We snakes of the world are divided into 15 families, 25 subfamilies and we do comprise of approximately 2500 species. There are nearly 3,000 species of us snakes in the world.

Out of these, only around 375 of us snake species are poisonous and venomous. Only a small proportion of these species are potentially harmful to the human kind.

Snakes That Live In The USA

Source: John Sullivan—Western Mud Snake

About twelve american people dye every year from poisonous and venomous snake bites. Our snake bites have just gotten even more deadly in America.

This is why kids and their parents must absolutely know some basic things about our species. Knowlege is the first step to survival and knowledge is power so let's look on the different species of us snakes that are living in the USA.

INTRIGUING FACT: ATTENTION SNAKE LOOKALIKE!

While it is not a snake, there is an animal that looks a good deal like us snakes. This giant oarfish can grow to lengths of over 50 feet long. This beautiful and strange animal is the likely origin of the sea serpent legends that you might heard of.

There are four different species of venomous snakes in the United States that you should be aware of.

These include the cottonmouth or water moccasin, the copperhead, the rattlesnake and the coral snake.

The Mojave rattlesnake is the most dangerous rattlesnake that lives in the United States.

However, there is another, much more potent snake than the rattlesnake that requires extra cautionary measures: the North American Coral snake.

Coral snakes are found primarily throughout the south-eastern United States, as well as in parts of Texas and Arizona.

Source: Dawson—North Florida Swamp Snake

Where Do Snakes Hang Out?

Source: Damien Farrell—Rainbow boas get their name from the coloration of their scales caused by iridescence

We snakes like to live in damp, dark, cool places where food exists in abundance. We snakes can live in a lot of different habitats like the deserts, the rain forests and even the oceans.

These are the types of places that we just love to hang around so be aware of these types of environments and especially if you are walking around in the dark. You should never walk alone and without a source of light.

Source: John Sullivan—Eastern Earth Snake John Sullivan

We love firewood stacked directly on the ground
　We love old lumber or junk piles
　We love gardens and flower beds with heavy mulch
　We love untrimmed shrubs and shrubs growing next to a foundation
　We love unmoved and unkempt lawns, abandoned lots and fields with tall vegetation
　We love pond and stream banks with abundant debris and trash
　We love cluttered basements and attics with a rodent, bird or bat problem
　We love feed storage areas in barn haylofts where rodents abound and
　We love to crawl into spaces under houses

Source: king snake—Calibas

INTRIGUING FACT ABOUT SNAKES: DID YOU KNOW THIS CURIOUS FACT ABOUT US SNAKES?
Snakes are found on every continent of the earth. There is only one exception to this rule. Snakes do not live in Antartica. Snakes do like to live and inhabit a big range of habitats. They live in the deserts, on mountains, in rain-forests, the savannah, forests that range from european to tropical forests and subtropical, and they even live in rivers, oceans, and streams. The snakes from around the world are divided into fivteen families and into twenty-five subfamilies. Snakes are comprised of approximately 2500 species.

There are just two countries that we snakes do not like to live on. These are the islands of Ireland and Bermuda. Have you noticed that both of these countries are islands?

Source: John Sullivan - Mississippi green water snake

The Anatomy Of Snakes

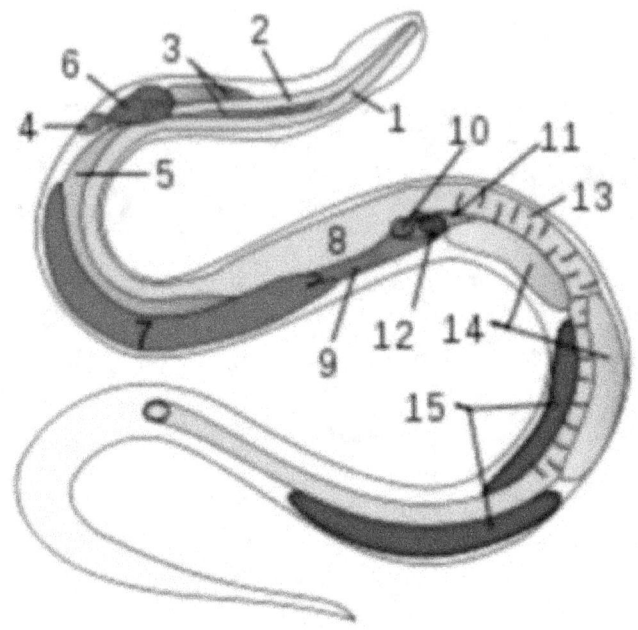

Source: Uwe Gille

1. Esophagus
2. Trachea
3. Tracheal lungs
4. Rudimentary left lung
5. Right lung
6. Heart
7. Liver
8. Stomach
9. Air sac
10. Gallbladder
11. Pancreas
12. Spleen
13. Intestine
14. Testicles
15. Kidneys

Source: Uwe Gille

The most noticeable physical characteristics of snakes include:
The lack of limbs.
No moveable eyelids.
No external ear openings.
An elongated body covered in scales, as opposed to hair or feathers.

The Skin: Scaly Skin

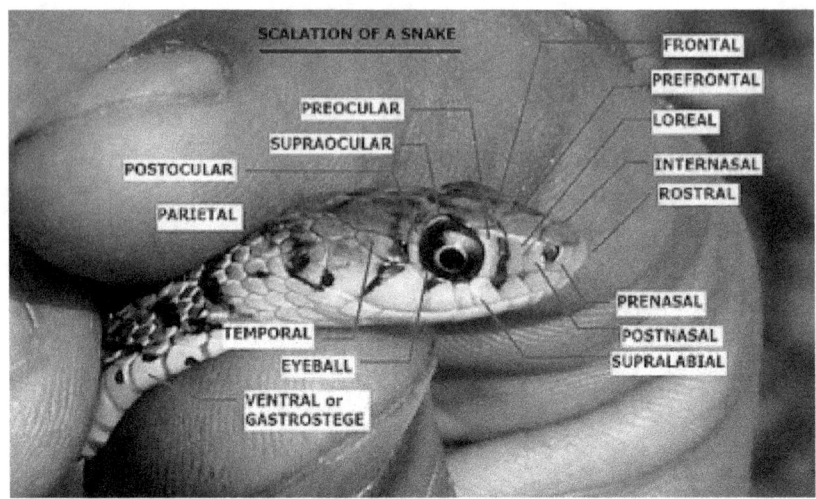

Source: AshLin—Nomenclature of scales (side view of head)
Scales on a snake's head

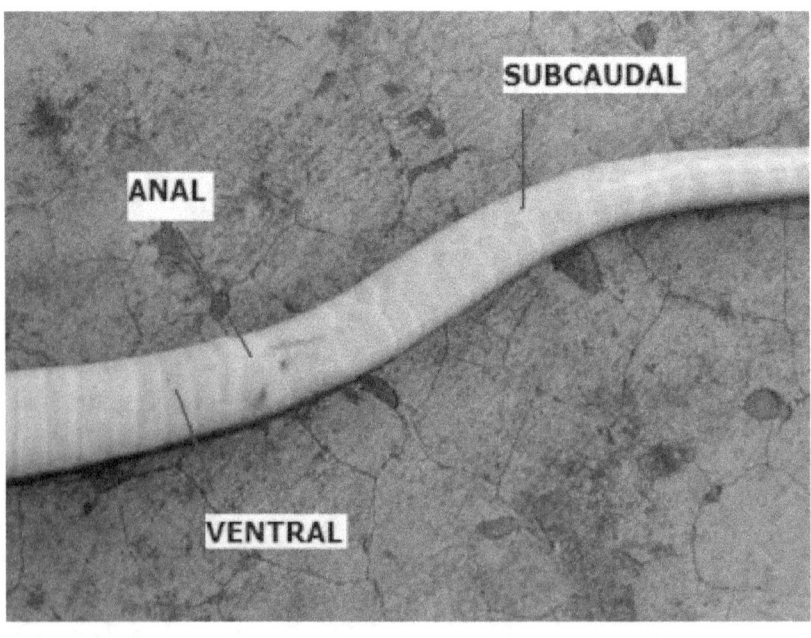

Source: AshLin—Ventral, anal, subcaudal scales on underside of a snake's body—Nomenclature of scales of a snake

INTRIGUING FACT ABOUT SNAKES: DID YOU KNOW THIS CURIOUS FACT ABOUT US SNAKES?

There are only 2 possible candidates that could claim the title of the largest snake of the world. 1. The Green Anaconda of central and tropical South America and 2. The Reticulated Python of Asia. Both can be classified as giants.

To the general public we snakes are simply viewed as a dangerous "slimy" cold-blooded abomination capable of inflicting serious bodily harm to the unsuspecting human victim.

This can not be farther from the truth as you will be able to learn in the upcoming chapters. Take a particular look at the chapter: "What is a snake's defence mechanism?" to learn the reasons why some of us snakes are venomous.

The Secrets Of A Snake's Skin

**Source: Peter Ellis— Diamond Python beginning a moult of its skin
The eye scales are visible as the moulting skin peels from the head first**

We snakes are going through a molting phase because we are outgrowing our skin and similar to a kid that grows taller. If a kid grows taller, he or she can not fit in the smaller clothing and needs to wear bigger sized clothing. Humans grow in height and have to adapt and we snakes outgrow our skin and we have to adapt, too.

We molt by rubbing ours head against something hard, causing the skin to split and regrow. We snakes will continue to rub until we are able to pull ourselves out of the old skin.

INTRIGUING FACT ABOUT SNAKES: DID YOU KNOW THIS CURIOUS FACT ABOUT US SNAKES?

The Reticulated Python (Python reticulatus) may achieve a maximum length of more than nince meter (29 feet). The longest reticulated Python ever recorded was 10.05 meter (33 feet). Despite this Python's impressive length, the record weight for a reticulated Python snake is 145 kilo (320 pounds). This is far less than the maximum weight of the Green Anaconda snake. As a result of its less bulkier and slender body, the reticulated Python is considered a far more agile snake.

Source: Srithern—Empty skin of a Snake

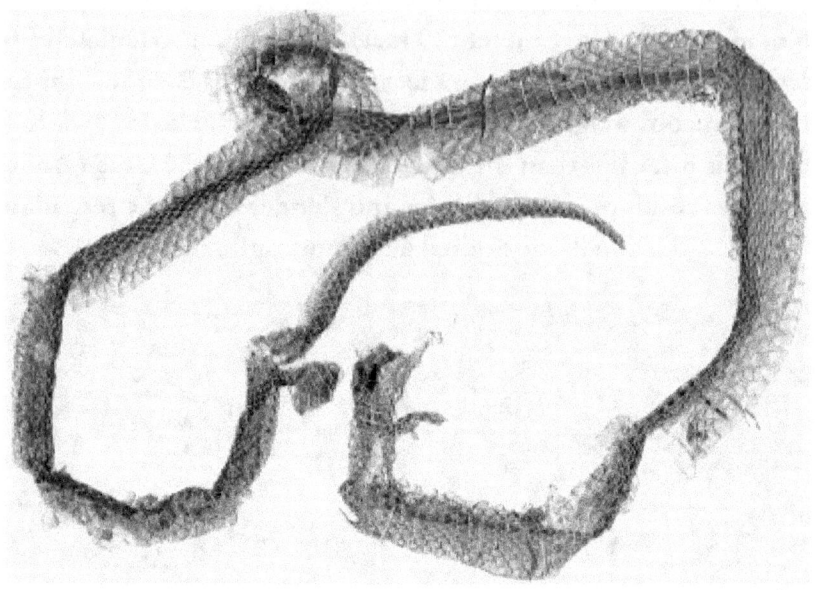

Source: Christian Fischer—Empty skin of a Grass Snake

We snakes and other reptiles as well (frogs, for example shed, too) shed our skin as part of the normal process of growing. Most of us snakes shed our skin four to eight times per year.

How often we snakes sheds our skin depends upon many factors, including the temperature of our environment, how often we eat, the amount we eat, the type of food we eat, and depending upon our activity level.

Our young snakes, for example, shed more frequently than older ones because like humans, snakes grow more rapidly in the first few years of life.

Source: Northern Water Snake shedding skin at Natural Bridge, Virginia

Do Snakes Have A 6th Sense?

Our sense organs are uniquely different than those of mammals and other animals. Unlike mammals, which mainly rely on their sight and hearing, we snakes rely primarily on our senses of smell and touch.

Some of us snakes also have a "sixth sense" that mammals and even other reptiles cannot boast. We snakes know when to stop squeezing because we do sense the heartbeats of our prey.

Eyes: We snakes do not have moveable eyelids, but transparent caps called "brille" as protective eye coverings. It's this missing feature that gives us this stare look that humans find so disconcerting. In many mammals, including humans, an unblinking stare is menacing, a sign of aggression, but we snakes really can't help it.

Our eyes do fit tightly in our head and we only have limited movement capabilities. We snakes do not see in color like humans do. Except for some of us snake species who are hunting with their eye sight. A sake's vision is unremarkable.

Ears: We snakes do not have external ears. We do lack an eardrum and some of the other internal structures common to mammals.

Nose: We snakes have a nose and nostrils that we draw air through. It's our first methodology of identifying smells, but it is not our only one because we are known for our 6 senses. We snakes also smell in an exceedingly different way than mammals.

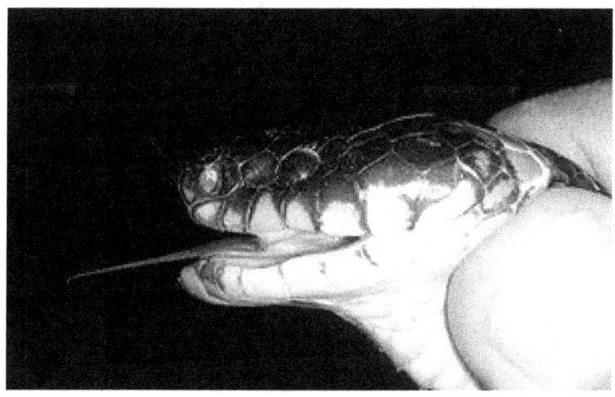

Source: AshLin—Banded Krait
captured in Binnaguri, North Bengal, India

Tongue:
We snakes (all of us) have a forked tongue. Do you know what's up with all that flicking in and out that we do? Well, as it turns out, we taste our environment, including us if we're nearby. We use our tongue to sample chemical molecules in the air which we draw into our mouth for identification by a special organ named the vomeronasal organ, or "Jacobson's organ."

Teeth:
All of us snakes have little tiny teeth, but they our teeth are not designed for gnawing. We are using them to hold prey, which is usually swallowed by us entirely.

Scaly skin:
Our skin is scaly and it is made of keratin. Keratin is one major ingredients in makeup, hair and nail care.

The same stuff that makes up the fingernails and hair of humans.

Our skin features a large spread of scaly skin types: Some types of us snakes have tiny and very soft scales. Some others do have overlapping scales and there are thoses who have scales that are keel-shaped and appear coarse while other scales are soft.

Movement:

If we snakes are cornered by a human being, we'll become scared and express our fear by hissing and shaking our tail. Besieged, we may advance as a bluff to shock the individual away. If that fails, we may finally strike. We snakes can strike about 1/2 of the length of its body length.

Mating, Snake Eggs & Snake Babies

We snakes do provide an interesting study group for mating experts because there are over three thousand species of us snakes around the world. Each species shows different mating tactics.

In order to bring our heritage to the next generation, mating takes place like this. Some of us female snakes lay eggs and others give birth to young ones.

When our femal snakes are ready to mate, she begins to release a special scent (pheromones) from her skin glands on her back.

As she goes about her daily routine, she leaves an odour trail as she pushes off resistance points on the ground. If one of us mature male snakes catches her scent, he will follow her trail until he finds her.

We male snakes begin to court the female snakes by bumping our chin on the back of her head and crawling over her. When she is willing, she raises her tail. At that point, we male snakes wrap our tail around hers so our tails meet at the cloaca.

INTRIGUING FACT ABOUT SNAKES: DID YOU KNOW THIS CURIOUS FACT ABOUT US SNAKES?

Mambas are a venomous snake specie that is found throughout Africa. This species is one of the deadliest snakes on earth. Worldwide Mambas and other venomous snake species kill more than 20,000 people per year

The female snakes reproduce about once or twice a year; however, the methods of birth vary among our many snake species. Some of the female snakes give birth to baby snakes (from one to 150 at a time), while our other snake species lay eggs (from one to 100 at a time).

Some of our female snakes even combine these two methods (hybrid method) by holding the eggs internally until they hatch, and the babies are born when they are already alive.

For the most part, our female snakes do not sit on their eggs like a hen, but in some cases our female snakes will protect their eggs (and their young) for a few days after having left the mother's body.

Our female snakes will reproduce, or give birth, once a year and in a cycle of every 3 years.

More Hatching Baby Snakes...

What Is A Snake's Defense Tactic?

Cycloid scales on Leptotyphlops humilis and other blind snake species are fluorescent, as a result when they are put under low frequency ultraviolet light (black light) they glow!

Venom is a common defence mechanism that some of our species are able to tap into for defense.

Venom itself is a poison secreted by animals for either defensive or offensive purposes. Venom originated from digestive enzymes that were originally located in the stomach.

There are also ways other than venom that snakes use to protect themselves.

Did you know that snake bites only happen as last resort of a snake's defence?

Camouflage

Although some of our skin patterns may appear vivid to the human eye, they effectively camouflage when we snakes are in our normal habitat.

We like to blend in with the background and therefore we tend to break up our outline so that nobody discovers and attacks us. We snakes may enhance this camouflage habit by our posture and movements.

Vine snakes, for example, do sway with the breeze, stick-mimics stay stiff.

INTRIGUING FACT ABOUT SNAKES: DID YOU KNOW THIS CURIOUS FACT ABOUT US SNAKES?

Did you know that the most venomous snakes are not the most dangerous snakes and not even the deadliest?

The Indian cobra is one of the most recognizable venomous snakes in the world.

Misdirection and head hiding

Some of us snakes do use our blunt tails to mimic the head, holding up, coiling or even striking out with our tails. Pipesnake's tails are flattened to resemble cobra hoods. In this case our real head is hidden within our coils, ready for a counterattack.

All of us snakes possess teeth that can be used in defensive bites. Most of us snakes rely on camouflage to avoid being seen, others coil up in a tight ball with the head in the middle, some rattle the tail, and a few of us even rub their scales together to produce a rasping **"leave me alone"** sound, but almost all of us snakes will flee if given even the slightest opportunity.

Other Snake Behaviors

Winter Dormancy:

In regions where winters are really col, we snakes can go into hibernation. Our hibernation is a bit different than that of mammals because mammals are actually asleep during hibernation. We are using a different method. When it is cold we are brumating. Brumating reptiles are awake and not asleep, but we are passive and do not entertain any activity during the brumating process. Some of us may brumate in burrows or under piles of rocks, while others brumate inside trees that are fallen on the ground.

Locomotion:

Our lack of limbs really does not impede our movements. We have developed different modes of locomotion depending on our environments. Unlike the gaits of limbed animals, which form a continuum, each different stage of snake locomotion is distinct and discrete from the others with very abrupt transitions that are happening between the different stages that happen during locomotion.

Lateral Undulation:

In the lateral undulation the body of us snakes flexes to our left and to our right. When we are doing the lateral undulation it looks like a wave.

Even though this movement seems to appear in a quick mode, we snakes rarely are moving quicker than 2 body lengths per second or less.

Rectilinear:

The slowest mode in that we are moving via locomotion is called rectilinear locomotion.

In this mode we can lift our belly scales and we can pull them forward. This kind of locomotion results in a series of ripples in our skin. Our large counterparts, the Pythons, often use this type of locomotion.

Vipers love it, too. Vipers love to apply this ninja locomotion tactic when they are looking and stalking prey.

Usually this happens across the open ground. Our snake buddies profit from this tactic because a snake's movements are very hard to identify by the prey because these movements happen in a very subtle way and this is exactly how it is done using the rectilinear trick!

Can Snakes Fly & Other Snake Specialities

Source: Mike Pingleton—Red Milk Snake

Are there snakes that can truly fly?

Well, the answer is a resounding yes we can. There does exist a species of us snakes in the jungles of South and Southeast Pacific Rim were flying snakes exist. Flying snakes flatten their bodies into a concave C shape to catch air as they fall. These species of us snakes can essentially make turns in the air, too!

A flying snake can't essentially gain altitude. These snakes are therefore gliders, utilising the speed of free fall and contortions of their bodies to catch the air and generate a lift. Flying snakes do not have wings neither.

How are they capable to fly then? Well, these snakes do 'fly ' by flattening their bodies from head to tail when they're in the air. A lot of them are about 3 to 4 feet long (1 to 1.2 meters).

INTRIGUING FACT ABOUT SNAKES: DID YOU KNOW THIS CURIOUS FACT ABOUT US SNAKES?

Yes Hognose Snakes are talented. These are great actresses and actors and they can fool even the smartest animals. They trick predators by using their playing dead act. Hognose Snakes can even set off rancid stench that will fool hungry flies.

Can some snakes eat rattlesnake?

Of course some of us can! Bull snakes or King snakes for example love to eat other snakes.

How do these snake look like:

A snake that can eat other snakes is up to 1,42 mm or 56 inches in total length with marks on the skin that change dependent on the snake's location the subspecies.

The scales are smooth and glossy and the pupils are round.

Habitat: This snake is located across the majority of Arizona. It is absent from Arizona's higher mountains and the high elevations of Mogollon Edge country.

In Arizona the Common King snake is present in biotic communities around desert scrubs.

Which are the snakes that eat other snakes?

Source: Dawson— Baby Western Coachwhip

There are a wide variety of us snakes that eat other elongate vertebrates, including other snakes. Familiar snake-eaters include the North American King snakes which have evolved resistance to the venom of many species of viper snakes.

Eastern Indigo Snakes and their Central and South American relatives are also frequent snake eaters, and many other species of North American colubrids sometimes dine on each other, including the Racers, Coachwhips, Garter and Ribbon Snakes, and Coral Snakes.

It is an arduous process, especially when we prey snakes are as long as or longer than our predator.

It's true: some of us snakes are able to ingest other snakes that equal or exceed their own body length. That means that these snakes must fit an object longer than their entire body into just their stomach, which is not as long as their whole body. Body width is not nearly as much as a problem because we snakes have highly kinetic skulls and very strong and flexible trunk muscles.

One of us snakes that famously feeds on other snakes is the king cobra.

Do Snakes live underwater?

Most of us snakes are really capable of staying underwater for periods. But water snakes and enormous stream snakes both can stay underwater much longer than average.

Since we snakes are exothermic (this means we get the heat from outside of our body not from inside like humans) and can do anaerobic cellular respiration, our energy and thus oxygen wants are much lower than average.

This lets us stay in warm tropical fresh or salt water for major amounts of time.

There are roughly 30-50 different sorts of sea snakes and they belong to the Cobra family.

Though all of us snakes can swim, sea snakes live generally in the water.

They do have to come up for air but can stay under water for at least an hour! Since they require air frequently they're generally found in shallow waters of the Indian Sea and hotter areas of the Pacific Sea.

These types of us snake species love to eat fish, fish eggs and eels that they find under rocks and in reefs.

Are there Snakes with horns?

Yes absolutely and they are called Cerastes or horned snakes.

These types of us snakes are little snakes, averaging less than 50 cm in length, but are comparatively stout in appearance.

Their head is wide, flat and distinct from the neck. The

Their head is covered with a supraorbital horn

This horn might be present over each eye in some of our snake species.

Found in the deserts of Northwards Africa and the Middle East, horned rattlesnakes are little, typically under 50 cm long.

They frequently have two horns over the eyes, but there are some of them that are lacking them totally, and, thus can be simply mistaken for other snakes.

They're toxic, but their bite is mostly non-fatal to humans.

INTRIGUING FACT ABOUT SNAKES: DID YOU KNOW THIS CURIOUS FACT ABOUT US SNAKES?

Sea Snakes are extremely venomous. They have the capability to kill 200 people. They love creating illusions to fool predators. I told you that we snakes are pretty sneaky! Yes, we snakes have a pretty tough reputation when it comes to tricks like creating illusions, playing dead, sniper tricks, and similar misleading tactics that involve disguising and camouflage!

What are the numerous Snakes with stripes?

Yes we snakes love our beautiful skin and some of us come with elegant striped skin. The number of stripes and color of stripes depends on the species.

Here are some beautiful striped species that you shoul be aware of:

Eastern Black-Neck Garter Snake

Source: Dawson—Blackneck Garter Snake

Bright orange stripe going down the back.

Checkered Garter Snake:

Thin white or yellow stripe down the back, encircled by checkerboard pattern of black spots.

Red Stripe Ribbon Snake

Source: Dawson—Redstripe ribbon snake

Dark red strip down back.

Texas Lined Snake:

It's got a pale stripe on an especially dark background with a faint row of spots on each side of the stripe.

Canebrake Rattlesnake:

An orange stripe of varied shades and width runs from head to tail often fading in the last 3rd bit of the snake. The tail is black or dark brown.

What Do Snakes Feed Upon?

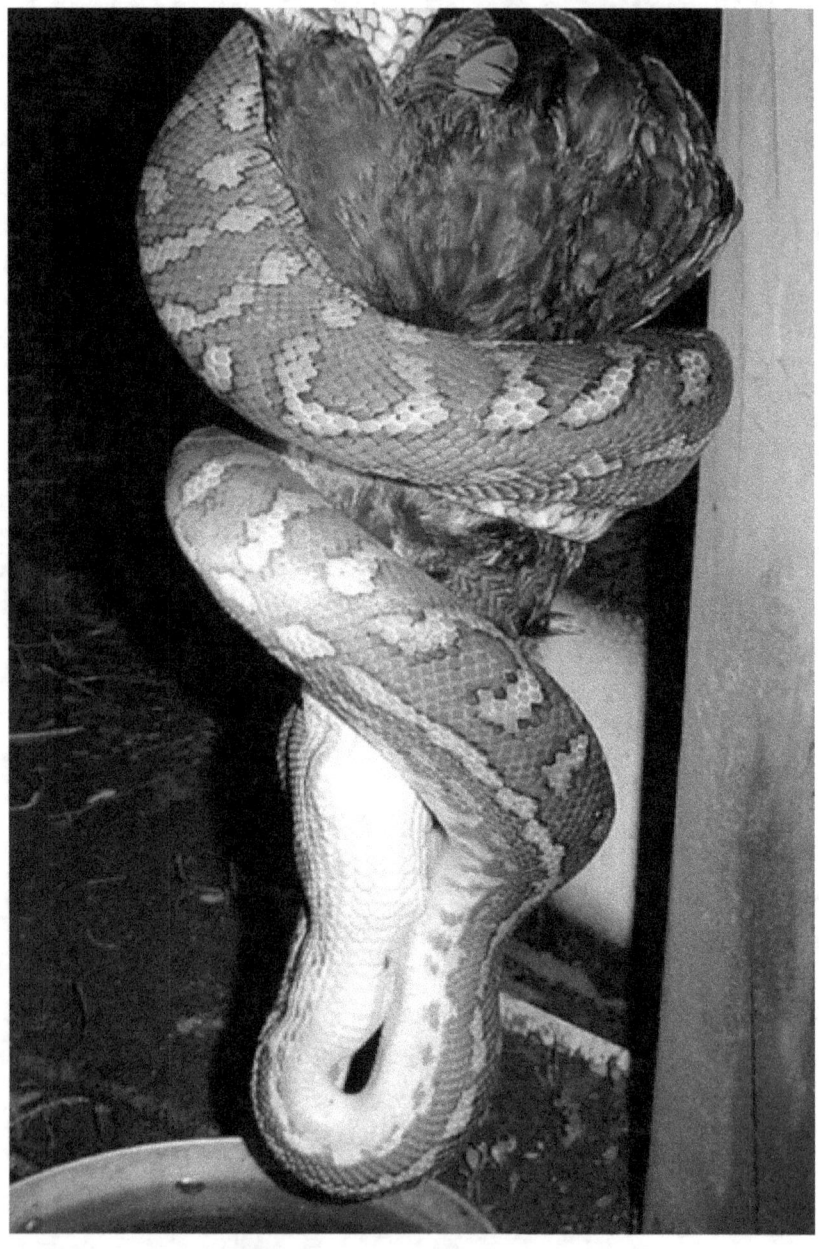

Source: Alikai—Carpet Snake eating a chicken

We snakes consume a variety of items including termites, rodents, birds, frogs, small deer and other reptiles.

We snakes also like to eat prey whole and are able to consume prey three times larger than the diameter of our heads because our lower jaw can separate from our upper jaw. To keep prey from escaping, we snakes have rear-facing teeth that hold our prey in our mouths.

INTRIGUING FACT ABOUT SNAKES: DID YOU KNOW THIS CURIOUS FACT ABOUT US SNAKES?

Very odd story. Did you know that there are records of snakes that are eating themselves? This behavior is called "Autophagy" in scientific terms. Some snakes will also eat other snakes' eggs. There is one particular species of snakes, the tentacled snake that also eats aquatic plants. This tentacled snake is the only snake that only likes to feed on green vegetation. This is a true vegan snake!

The venomous and poisonous snakes that are part of our heritage do inject prey with venom, while constrictors squeeze the prey. They do not need to hunt for food every day.

Anacondas and pythons, for example, can survive for up to one year without food after feeding.

What you should be aware of is that we snakes love to hund mostly at night and that is why you should not go out alone into nature at night and without lighting.

Eastern Cottonmouth

Do Snakes Have Predators?

Source: Benny Mazur—Midland Brown Snake

While many of us snake creatures snack on snakes as a side dish and when we are hungry, we are only afraid of a few predators that catch us as prey.

These are the exceptions: some birds who are able to catch us as prey and some particular snake species that are snake eaters.

INTRIGUING FACT ABOUT SNAKES: DID YOU KNOW THIS CURIOUS FACT ABOUT US SNAKES?

Did You know that there are no venomous constrictors? Yes, it is true. These snakes kill via constrictions.

They are very good swimmers. They have established populations on many relatively remote islands within their range. Fishermen often report seeing these types of snakes very far from the land. Apparently, they are living completely at ease in the ocean.

Until recently these types of snakes were much more common. Today, their numbers have been declining.

These snakes are primarily ambush hunters.

Birds are major snake predators. I am not only talking about just regular birds, but there are some little itty bitty birds who love to eat baby snakes.

Some birds specialize in snakes. Small snakes are vulnerable to other bigger carnivorous or omnivorous creatures. Even spiders eat small and juvenile snakes. Some spider do even have venom to kill small pit vipers.

Sadly enough, the most efficient and widespread predator of snakes is the human kind because some humans are intentionally killing snakes for various reasons. Please look at the chapter "How Bad Are Snakes Endangered" to learn more about this subject.

It is true, humans have killed more of us snakes and destroyed our snake habitats in a way that no other snake predator has done it.

The 10 Most Venomous Snakes

Southern Copperhead

Rattlesnake

The rattlesnakes, for example, get their name from the rattle at the end of their tail, a feature that separates them from all of us other snake species. This rattle is composed of changed, epidermal scutes-dry, hollow, loosely overlapping segments made up of keratin, the same material that makes up our nails. A rattlesnake's rattle is built like a pile of little, interlocking cup-like structures. When the snake shakes its tail, the segments bump against one another making a humming sound like the sound of grease sizzling in a pan.

New-born rattlesnake snakes don't have their rattle yet and it will be developed over time and as they grow. This process usually takes a process of several months before the young rattler can generate a soft rattle.

Some people believe one can tell the age of a rattlesnake by counting the number of rattle segments in its rattle.

INTRIGUING FACT ABOUT SNAKES: DID YOU KNOW THIS CURIOUS FACT ABOUT US SNAKES?

What is venom?
Venom is a cocktail. This venom cocktail consists of 100 of different enzymes and proteins.
A big majority of these enzymes and proteins are pretty harmless to the human being. However, a tiny percentage of these ingredientsare toxins. There are roughly 20 types of different toxic enzymes in venomous snake species. The majority of venomous snakes only employ six to twelve of these toxins. No single venomous snake species employs all of these 20 toxins at the same time.

Death Adder

Death Adders, another of us snake species, are the most discernible snakes in Australia. They have the practice of burying themselves in sand or leaf litter, with just their head and tail exposed while they lurk for potential prey. When a little bird, lizard or little mammal approaches, they twitch their tail speedily like a grub to draw in their prey.

If the prey approaches close enough, the speedy strike barely misses its mark. Their practice of lying still, partly exposed, makes them hard to see and easier stepped on.

It is a deadly snake with a thick body and a flat, triangular head. There are way more than 180 species in the death adder family.

Some are ordinarily called adders.

Viper

Vipers typically live on the ground, but some live in trees. They eat frogs, lizards, and tiny mammals and birds.

The Europen Viper or common Viper has been located from Great Britain to Southeast East Asia and in the Arctic Circle.

It is pale gray to yellow with a dark brown line down its back. It grows to a length of 2 feet. Its bite isn't deadly to humans. Russell's viper snakes, found in India, Sri Lanka, and Thailand, reach a length of approximately 4 feet. It is tan, blue, and black with geometrical marks on its back. Its bite is perilous.

The Gaboon viper of Africa is the biggest of the viper snakes, reaching a length of six 0.5 feet (2 meters). It is yellowish with 3 rows of oval, dark-ringed spots on its body. Its fangs are 2 inches (5 cm) longer than those of another snake.

Its bites are very dangerous.

Philippine Cobra

Indian Cobra—Source: Gregor Younger

The northerly Philippine Cobra is a squat, awfully poisonous snake local to the Philippines.

They're found on the Luzon, Mindoro, Catanduanes and Masbate islands.
Its average length is 1,70 meter.

Populations from Mindoro Island are thought to be up to two meters in length.

Its color is light to medium brown while the young cobra's color is a darker brown.

They have 23 to 20 scale rows round the neck and 21 just above the middle area of the body.

They prey on mice, frogs and tiny mammals. The female lays eggs in clutches of 10 to 20 with an incubation time of 60 to 70 days.

Tiger Snake

Source: JAW—Tiger Snake

The common tiger snake is present in southern and eastern Australia.

They're generally around one meter long and have a striped marking (thus the name Tiger Snake).

This isn't always true nevertheless as the marks can change because of the seasons and the age of the snake.

They can grow up to 1.5 metres in length.

These are toxic snakes and they will attack if they're ruffled or threatened. Otherwise, they can live noiselessly.

They also are frequently territorial, and will live in the same area for a while. They're also found in suburban areas, even in the more recent suburbs.

These snakes eat all sorts of creatures. They cheerily eat frogs, fish, little birds and other little mammals.

They also eat other reptiles like lizards.

Black Mamba

**Source: Bill Love/Blue
Chameleon Ventures Black mamba in defensive posture**

The Black Mamba is the most devastating snake on the planet. They grow fourteen feet long and can travel at a velocity of at least twelve miles per hour.
They've a head formed like a coffin.

The Black Mamba isn't essentially black. They've a brownish-grey body with a light belly and brownish scales along its back. It gets its name from the color of the liner of its mouth, which is purple-black, and which it displays when threatened.

The Black Mamba lives in the country of South Africa.

Black Mambas like open and low habitats like savannahs, rocky places and open woods. They're active in the daytime.

They regularly sleep in hollow trees, burrows, rock clefts, or empty termite mounds.

Black Mambas will come back to the same place each night.

The Black Mambas eat tiny mammals and birds, like voles, rats, squirrels, mice, rats, or bush babies.

INTRIGUING FACT ABOUT SNAKES: DID YOU KNOW THIS CURIOUS FACT ABOUT US SNAKES?

Black Mambas are aggressive cratures and they are the fastest snakes on earth, too. They can achieve a maximum speed of up to 23 km/h. They are so aggressive that if you get within 23 m into their privacy zone, they will charge themselves and strike up to a dozens of times in a row, injecting more and more venom each time and in order to defend themselves.

Taipan

Taipans are extremely deadly snakes.

They're exceedingly long snakes at the same time.

They live in the hot north part of Australia. They eat rats, birds, lizards and tiny animals.

Australia has thirty different types of poisonous (deadly) snakes.

The biggest and most deadly of them is the taipan (correct pronunciation is tie-pan).

It is in truth said to be doubtless the most poisonous snake internationally.

The taipan grows to over 2.5 metres in length. There are 2 species, or kinds, of taipan snakes.

Blue Krait

Source: Wibowo Djatmiko (Wie146)—Blue krait, ca. 70cm
Karawang, West Java

The blue krait, sometimes called the Malayan krait, is a very highly toxic but common species that lives in Peninsular Malaysia, Thailand, Singapore and Sumatra in Southeast Pacific Rim.

It exists in lowland to upper-level rainforest across the Peninsular, including its surrounding islands. This species has broad black bands across a white body, infrequently with yellowish patches.

It feeds essentially on snakes and skinks in natural settings.

Of the 'Big Four' threatening snakes found in India, the Common Krait is the most poisonous. Its venom - a dynamic neurotoxin - is meant to be 15 times more aggressive than that of the Common Cobra, making it doubtless the most poisonous snake in The East and earning a top listing among the deadliest snakes of our world!

Eastern Brown Snake

Large Eastern Brown Snake

Eastern Brown Snake bites from this species have caused human deaths.

Actually the Eastern Brown Snake accounts for more deaths than any other Australian Snake.

A scared, prepared biter it'll protect itself if threatened. It maintains a powerful defensive "S" formed posture. It is exceedingly variable in coloration and pattern. Color goes from pale tan through orange, russet, dark brown & just about black, occasionally with cross-body banding.

Hatchling and minors especially change in color, often having dark heads or neck bands, or being utterly banded along the body length.

Fierce Snake or Inland Taipan

Source: AllenMcC.— Olive colored Fierce Snake

The Fierce Snake or the Inland Taipan can reach a total length of 2.5 metres, though 1.8 metres is the more common length.

The higher surface of the snake can vary widely from dark brown to a light straw color.

Dramatic seasonal color changes occur, with a darker winter and lighter summer coloration.

These changes are an adaption to the tough outback climate, the darker marks soaking up heat more effectively in winter and the reverse in summer.

The cruel snake resides in the black soil fields in the area where Queensland, South Australia and the North Territory borders meet up.

Their diet is virtually only composed from tiny mammals, especially local rats, which, at certain times reach plague proportions in this area.

16 Non-Venomous Snakes

Brown Water Snake

Source: BirdPhotos.com—Brown Water Snake, West Palm Beach, Florida.

It's a big corpulent, brown, patterned snake with eyes nearly on top of its head. These fish-eaters climb well, and are ordinarily seen luxuriating on tree branches hanging above the Canoochee and Ogeechee Brooks.

It bites only if attacked and swims underwater speedily to flee.

Banded Water Snake

The Banded Water Snake is a snake with a faint banded pattern over a dark coloured background of black, brown, or red. They are also called "water bandits". These snakes are extraordinarily abounding snakes living in grassy ditches, swamps, pools, streams, and streams.

They swim well and frequently dive underwater. Frogs and fish are their first prey.

These snakes are ill-tempered and bite if handled.

Mud snakes

A Mud Snake is a large (up to 6 feet), smooth and shiny snake that is aquatic and lives in swamps, ponds, and marshes. This handsome black-and-orange snake eats sirens and amphiumas (large eel-like salamanders). Mud snakes are often killed by vehicles as they cross roads, moving between swamps on stormy nights.

Eastern Indigo Snake

This snake is federally guarded by the Endangered Animals Act. It's the biggest snake in the US, reaching up to 8.6 feet long, and 10 lbs. in weight.

This bluish-black snake frequently has some orange-red pigment on the jaw and neck.

They often shelter in tortoise burrows and have territories including masses of acres.

Indigo snakes are acquiescent, almost never biting animals, but are forceful predators known to consume tiny turtles, rats, frogs, cottonmouths, and rattlesnakes.

Scarlet King Snake

Source: Glenn Bartolotti—Adult Scarlet King Snake, Florida

A reasonably tiny (up to 2 feet) and stunning snake ringed with red, yellow or white, and black.

This snake is not unusual to abounding in pine flat woods habitats around the south-eastern regions of Georgia in the US.

The flattened snout is probably an adaptation for squeezing beneath bark.

Scarlet king snakes are often found under the bark of pine snags; they shed their skins and find prey (green anoles) in this habitat.

It is a secretive animal that prowls at night during the summer.

Scarlet Snake

This is yet another fairly small (up to 2 feet) red, black, and white snake which somewhat resembles the venomous coral snake. Scarlet snakes have a red snout and a series of red blotches or spots, outlined by black. This is a very common snake that burrows in sandy habitats. It is secretive and seldomly encountered by human beings.

Corn Snake

Source: Corn Snake

Also called the "red rat snake". A commonplace snake (up to 4 feet) in southern Georgia, the corn snake is a colorful animal with red, black-bordered smears on an orange background. The belly scales possess a bold, checkerboard or "piano key" pattern.

This enticing snake is a muscly constrictor that is extremely capable of climbing high in pursuit of bird nests. It frequently crosses roads after sundown in the summer.

Prey includes rats, mice, birds, and their eggs. Young corn snakes eat lizards.

Eastern Kingsnake

Source: Dawson

Long a fave among snake-enthusiasts, this species usually reaches about five feet long. The eastern kingsnake has a chain-like pattern of white or cream marks on a black or blackish-green background.

Like many snakes, kingsnakes regularly move or hunt in wet weather preceding a tempest. One engaging local name for this snake is "swamp-thumper"!

This strong constrictor eats frogs, rats, and snakes.

It frequently consumes toxic snakes and is impervious to their venom.

Eastern Coachwhip

Source: Hunter Desportes—Eastern coachwhip

Golden and platted like a rope, this snake is extraordinarily slim, but exceedingly long.

Coachwhips reach up to 7.5 feet long, making them one of the longest snakes in the U. S.!

These fast-paced "lizard chasers" inhabit sandy, piney habitats called sandhills. These snakes are active in the daytime.

They occasionally climb trees chasing baby birds and are known to eat baby snakes.

Black Racer

Simply one of the most typical snakes in southeast Georgia, the smooth racer is frequently seen zipping across roads throughout the day.

This black snake is fast-paced with adults generally 3-4 feet long.

It is quicker, much "skinner", and significantly commoner than the protected eastern indigo snake.

Indigos generally have some orange-red on the jaw and throat, racers have a white jaw.

Racers eat mice, rats, frogs, and other snake.

Rough Green Snake

**Source: cc-by-sa-2.5—Rough Green Snake, draped over vegetation
Location: Durham County, North Carolina, United States**

This species is linked with densely vegetated areas having vines, bushes and plants.

They're frequently faced along the perimeters of streams and lakes. They frequently climb foliage in pursuit of prey, feeding on spiders, grasshoppers, and other invertebrates.

Adults are extraordinarily slim and infrequently reach lengths of more than 3 feet. This is the sole "green" snake in Georgia, USA. They're harmless and don't bite.

Eastern Hognose Snake

Source: Bladerunner8u—Eastern Hognose Snake in southern Georgia, USA

This species is characteristically found in sandy uplands, including mixed oak-pine forests and pine flatwoods.

The best identifying feature of Hognose Snakes is the upturned muzzle.

The eastern hognose snake feeds basically on toads.

They use their specialized lengthened teeth in the back of the jaw. These teeth are used to "pop" toads and expedite swallowing.

This species is noted for an impressive defensive display that includes hissing and spreading the neck cobra-like.

If pestered further, they will roll over on their back and play dead.

Ringneck Snake

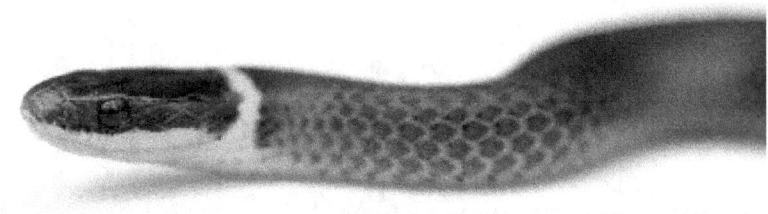

Source: Brian.gratwicke—Ringneck Snake

This species is limited to clammy environments. It happens in pine or deciduous forests with heavy ground litter.

It's a highly private species. These snakes grow to lengths of a little more than one foot. They're eaten by many other sorts of snakes including coral snakes. They do not bite humans.

Redbelly Snake

This species is in damp wood areas with abounding ground litter and like the ring neck snake this snake is commonly found in suburban areas. It is slim and reaches a length of one foot.

Red-bellied snakes feed generally on slugs and earthworms. Red snakes may exhibit strange defence behavior when picked up. They curl their higher lips upwards, making their mouths look bigger, but they never bite humans.

Eastern Garter Snake

Source: Eastern Garter Snake in Spangler Park, Wooster, Ohio

This species is found in a diversity of grassy habitats that are usually wet or damp, although not necessarily near permanent aquatic areas.

This snake is a large specimen and it can occasionally reach a length of greater than 3 feet.

Garter snakes have black lines on their lip scales, whereas ribbon snakes do not.

This species gives birth to sometimes more than 50 babies at a time.

Common garter snakes feed on earthworms, frogs, toads, salamanders, fish and tadpoles.

Eastern Ribbon Snake

Source: Eastern Ribbon Snake

These snakes are usually found near aquatic areas, particularly along lake or swamp margins.

The species is more slender than the garter snake, but it is otherwise similar in general appearance.

Ribbon snakes usually are less than 2 feet in length, although occasionally individuals may reach 3 feet.

Eastern ribbon snakes feed on salamanders, frogs and small fish.

The 10 Most Beautiful Snakes On Earth

Green Tree Python

The Green Tree Python is a colourful green colored snake, but some adult Tree Pythons may be colored in blue or yellow.

They have got a series of white or blue dorsal and / or lateral spots obvious in most.

The hatchlings are very variable in color from brick red to lemon yellow to brown.

Weirdly enough, all these colors can be discovered in the same clutch.

Habitat: wet, warm tropical regions

Diet in natural settings: little rodents (mice, rabbits) and birds.

Honduran Milk snake

Source: Haplochromis—Honduran milk snake, taken at the Zoo in Berlin, Germany

Honduran milk snakes were first imported to the U.S. about the late 70s or early 80s.

This snake has an indisputable beauty! Don't you agree?

Leucistic Texas Rat Snake

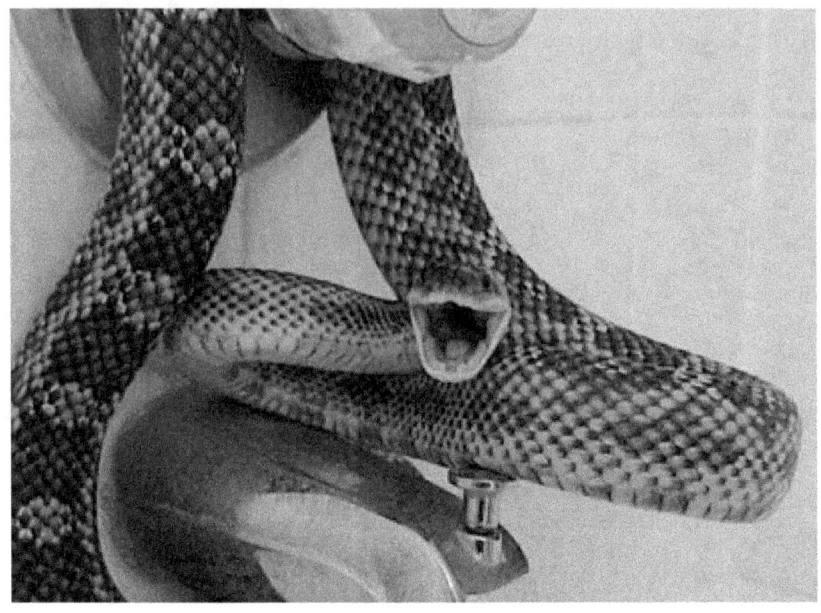

Source: Dawson—Texas Rat Snake

The Texas rat snake is a fairly big snake capable of attaining lengths past six feet.

They change considerably in color and patterning all though their range, but they're sometimes yellow or tan in color, with brown to olive-green, irregular smearing from head to tail.

The Texas rat snake has an insatiable appetite, consuming many rodents and birds, and infrequently lizards and frogs which they subdue with constriction.

They're generalists, found in a large range of habitats from swamps, to forests to grasslands, even in built up areas.

Indigo Eastern Rat Snake

The Indigo Eastern Rat Snake is the longest Northern US snake. Glossy black- or bluish-black in color, the snake has a black, kind of red or brownish jaw. The hatchlings are 19-24 inches long (48 - 61 cm) and might have yellow colouring on their body's forepart.

Both adult and young have sizeable, smooth scales in seventeen rows and a single anal plate.

The Emerald Tree Boa

Source: Jyothis—Emerald Tree snake in the Baltimore National Aquarium

The Emerald Tree Boa has a big, chunky head that's obviously distinguished from the much thinner neck. The back of the head is outlined by 2 pretty large bulges on both sides that make a contribution to the bulkiness of the head.

The eyes have pupils that are thin and vertically orientated like those of a kitty.

They have many heat receptors that are also present in most bodies.

These heat receptors pick up infrared radiation and essentially give the snake a picture of the thermo-environment around them.

Amelanistic Burmese Python

The Amelanistic Burmese Python is the biggest subspecies of the Indian Python and one of the 6 biggest snakes globally. It is local to a massive change of tropic and sub-tropic areas of Southern and Southeast Far East, including eastern India, Nepal, Western Bhutan, Southeast Bangladesh, Myanmar, Thailand, Laos, Cambodia, Vietnam, northwards continental Malaysia, Southern China and in Indonesia on Java, Southern Sulawesi, Bali, and Sumbawa.

This python is a brilliant swimmer and requires a permanent source of water.

It can be found in grasslands, marshes, swamps, rocky foothills, woodlands, river valleys, and jungles with open clearings.

Pythons are good climbers and have prehensile tails.

Brazilian Rainbow Boa

Source: Angela Rothermann—Rainbow Boa

Brazilian Rainbow Boas are slim bodied snakes that average between 5-7 feet long. They're possibly one of the prettiest snakes worldwide.

Brazilian Rainbow Boas generally range all the way from deep red to bright orange.

They've also got bold crescent moons on their side that contrast their dazzling color.

If captivated they essentially eat mice and rats that are nearly as thick as the widest part of their body.

Brazilian Rainbow Boa babies are sufficiently big enough to eat hopper mice and pink rats.

Eastern Coral Snake

Source: Norman.benton—Micrurus fulvius, Eastern Coral Snake, Jacksonville, Florida

The Eastern Coral Snake has a color pattern that is composed of a collection of rings that encircles the body: wide red and black rings parted by narrow yellow rings.

The head is black from the rostral to just behind the eyes.

The red rings are sometimes spotted with black.

Human beings who live in its natural range are usually taught a rhyme that they learn at a very young age:

"Red touches black, chum of Jack, red touches yellow, kill a fellow."

Nevertheless, this rhyme is only pertinent to the North American species, and cannot be used reliably in the Caribbean, or Central or South America.

Blue Racer Snake

Source: Patrick Coin—Northern Black Racer, Durham County North Carolina, United States

The Blue Racer snake is a gun-metal gray snake with a definite greenish cast. Nevertheless, interbreeding frequently happens in the area where the populations of the black and blue racer overlap, leading to the blue and black racer intergrade.

The blue racer happens in western Ohio. A diagonal line drawn across the state from Hamilton County to Ashtabula County would approximately mark the area where the populations of the black and blue racer overlap.

The Most Endangered Snakes On Earth

The San Francisco Garter Snake

Source: self2—San Francisco garter snake

The San Francisco Garter snake has a wide dorsal stripe of greenish yellow, rimmed in black, bordered by a red stripe, then black again. Its belly is bright turquoise. Due to its red stripe, the Red-sided Garter snake is often confused with the San Francisco Garter snake. Adult size ranges up to three feet.

The San Francisco Garter Snake is a slim snake.

Habitat: They stay near water, pools, streams, marshes or perhaps ditches. When scared, it'll swim away.

If caught, it'll beat around and bite and expel the contents of its glands on its attacker.

Breeding: They reproduce in the spring or autumn and the females give birth to snake babies in July through Aug. A female San Francisco Garter Snake can give birth to up to two dozen of babies at the same time.

The San Francisco Garter Snake is designated (since 1967) as an endangered subspecies.

Eastern Indigo Snake

Source: Eastern indigo snake

The Eastern Indigo is the biggest snake local to the U. S.. It's been on the Endangered Wildlife list since 1978 due to eradication of habitat.

The food prey of the Eastern Indigos include other snakes (toxic snakes as well), frogs, toads, infrequently birds, and tiny mammals.

It isn't a constrictor and just clings to its prey with its strong jaws.

These are extremely active snakes and are as sure to be out in the daytime as during the night.

Breeding occurs in mid-winter, with 6-10 eggs being laid in the late spring.

Babies hatch at close to a foot long and may reach maturity with the age of three years.

The biggest Eastern Indigo measured almost 9 feet long.

A more common size for this snake is 6 feet.

This snake was put on the U.S. endangered species list of snakes in the year of 1971.

The King Cobra

Source: Hari Prasad—A King Cobra in captivity
Dr. Aithal's Snake park, Puttur

The King Cobra is the biggest toxic snake globally.

They have the most perilous venom, but they inject amounts that'd be deadly to a full-grown elephant or about twelve adult humans.

It hangs on to its prey all in one bite or multiple 'chewings'!

The King Cobra can reach eighteen feet (over five meters) in length and can move with its head upright.

It can stand over 5 feet high (one in three of its length).

It can spray venom and if attacked will shoot at the eyes / face of its prey.

The range of the King Cobra includes India, the Philippines, Malaysia, Southeast Far East and southern China.

They live in heavy-forested areas and eat other poisonous snakes as well as lizards and frogs.

Due to its private and wary nature, King Cobras are infrequently seen.

The world wide mortality rate from bites is 2 or 3, significantly less than other toxic species.

They'd rather leave than fight, but are swift and assertive when incited.

The King Cobra is also a holy symbol in several cultures.

Kind Kobras might become endangered very soon if humans keep continuing killing them at the current rate.

Dumeril's Boa

Boa dumerili

The Dumeril's Boa, that is moderately found in the pet industry in the US, is located naturally only in the dry south-western end of the island of Madagascar.

It's a smaller member of the boa family, infrequently reaching more than six feet, with females being bigger than males.

The babies are born bigger than would be predicted for a boa of this size, at 20-24 inches.

The Dumeril's Boa is a ground-dwelling species that preys on little mammals and reptiles.

The elimination of Madagascar's forests for farming has left this boa very vulnerable.

This snake is yet another endangered species. Only about ten percent of Boa Dumerili's are alive in Madagascar's forests.

Some conservation organizations are helping with their initiative to preserve Madagascar's nature reserves and wildlife.

Snakes As Pets

We snakes may also be kept as a pet in the house with special focus upon their food. Feeding us snakes can be hideous, academic and educational at the same time.

We snakes eat our prey entirely by unhinging our jaw and swallowing it. Since you manifestly can't go to a food store and pick up some chicken legs, you've got to make certain to feed us snakes the correct prey.

Source: FelixReimann—Rat Snake

It is true that many of us snake species make attractive, exotic, and interesting pets. One of our species, the corn snake, for example, is the most popular reptile pet found in the world.

Other snakes of our species can be very skittish and turn out to be more aggressive than the pet owner might have anticipated. Bites, however, are seldom serious with us pet snakes.

Dawson—Smooth Earth Snake

Like nearly all colubrids, our buddies, the rat snakes, for example, do not present a threat to the pet keeper.

Rat snakes were long thought to be completely nonvenomous by pet snake experts, but recently they found out that some of our "old world" species do in fact have some small amounts of venom. These amounts are so tiny so that the issue becomes negligible.

However, before getting a pet snake you should always talk to the person or the shop keeper from where you are planning to get the snake in order to inform yourself personally about the harms that come with the specific type of specie that you want to keep as a pet snake.

Never rely on one single source of information because we snakes truly must be understod and studied before one is capable of caring for us pet snakes.

Make sure to understand all the dangers, risks, harms, and other issues that might come up with us pet snakes.

You should read many books, watch many educational films and documentaries, and talk to people who are in contact with us pet snakes themselves.

You should also be aware of the many species and differences of us non venomous snakes. Make sure to understand what species of us snakes are legally allowed as pets so that you can judge for yourself and know the exact differences.

Knowing the truth and having the knowledge about us snakes is the basis for such a pet snake project.

How To Prevent Snake Bites?

Source: Piet Spaans—Vipera berus male

It is always important to correctly identify the secies prior to picking it up or handling it.

Many accidents have occured as a result of misidentification (personal experience included), and quite honestly......it's not worth the risk. xxxxxxxx

If you are outside in the nature make sure you never go out in the wild. Let an adult help you and never go out to experience an adventure on your own. Never leave your save trail and go into the wild or into the woods alone without any support from an adult.

Do not go out alone in the dark and without a proper source of lighting. You should always be accompanied by an adult at night. The night time is not a good time for adventures or for leaving a trail into the unknown.

If you are out in the nature with adults and friends make sure that you are wearing long heavy pants and shoes with leather reinforcement. This clothing will help protect you from snake bites. Avoid tall grasses, thick marshy areas and areas that are known snake habitat.

INTRIGUING FACT ABOUT SNAKES: DID YOU KNOW THIS CURIOUS FACT ABOUT US SNAKES?

The Spitting Cobra is very sneaky because it can defends itself by spitting. If attacked, the spitting cobra can spit its venom from 3.4 meters away to target the predator.

Never put your hands in places where you can't see what you are touching. If you see a snake, leave it alone and give it plenty of room to escape.

If you get bitten, seek immediate medical attention.

General symptoms of Snakebite

Central
- Dizziness
- Fainting
- Increased thirst
- Headache

Systemic
- Fever
- Severe pain

Respiratory
- Breathing difficulty

Wound site
- Bleeding
- Fang marks
- Discoloration
- Burning sensation
- Swelling

Other skin sites
- Bleeding spots
- Numbness
- Tingling
- Sweating

Vision
- Blurriness

Heart and vessels
- Rapid pulse
- Low blood pressure
- Severe shock

Muscular
- Convulsions
- Loss of coordination
- Weakness

Gastric
- Nausea
- Vomiting

Intestinal
- Diarrhea

Curious Stuff About Snakes

African egg-eating snake

Begin to uncover the mysteries of the snakes from around the world. Unlock their secret. Always remember as you are in your discovery phase that snakes are often misunderstood creatures by human beings!

Instead, we humans should look at them with a fresh pair of eyes because snakes have been able to survive throughout evolution because of their adaptability capabilities.

This animal's heritage is millions of years old and we humans can learn a few things from such a smart and wise animal.

Below you will find many other intriguing, curious, and amazing facts that you might have ignored yourself about these graceful, beautiful, highly specialized, smart, wise, and adapted animals...

Most Intriguing Facts About Snakes ...

Snakes are carnivores (meat eaters).

Snakes don't have eyelids.

Snakes can't bite food so have to swallow it whole.

Snakes have flexible jaws which allow them to eat prey bigger than their head!

Snakes are found on every continent of the world except Antarctica.

Snakes have internal ears but not external ones.

Snakes used in snake charming performances respond to movement, not sound.

There are around 3000 different species of snake.

Snakes have a unique anatomy which allows them to swallow and digest large prey.

Source: Tie Guy II - Northern Brown Snake

Most Intriguing Facts About Snakes...

Snakes are covered in scales.

Snakeskin is smooth and dry.

Snakes shed their skin a number of times a year in a process that usually lasts a few days.

Some species of snake, such as cobras and black mambas, use venom to hunt and kill their prey. Read more venomous snake facts.

Snakes smell with their tongue.

Pythons kill their prey by tightly wrapping around it and suffocating it in a process called constriction.

Some sea snakes can breathe partially through their skin, allowing for longer dives underwater.

Anacondas are large, non-venomous snakes found in South America that can reach over 5 m (16 ft.) in length.

Source: Dawson

Myths & Truths About Snakes

Myths & Facts About Snakes...

Myth: Rat Snakes are poisonous.

Fact: Rat snakes are Non-poisonous, rodent-eating Reptiles.

Myth: Rat Snakes mate with cobras.

Fact: Rat Snakes or any other snakes will not mate with any snake out of its own species. Cobras eat other snakes so a mating between a Cobra and a Rat snake is not possible.

Myth: Snakes drink Milk.

Fact: Snakes drink water and do not drink milk; neither can they digest it properly. They are reptiles and have no association with milk, only mammals that have mammary glands can produce milk and thus a liking for milk in non-mammals is unlikely. But in a crises when severely dehydrated, a snake might drink any liquid available.

Myth: Some Snakes grow a beard as they get older.

Fact: Snakes are reptiles and do not have any hair on their bodies let alone a beard. It is impossible for them to have beards for their bodies do not have any ability of growing hair.

Myth: Snakes carry a diamond in their forehead.

Fact: It is impossible for a Snake to carry anything in its head. The mythological status attached with a Snake in India is probably responsible for this myth.

Myths & Facts About Snakes ...

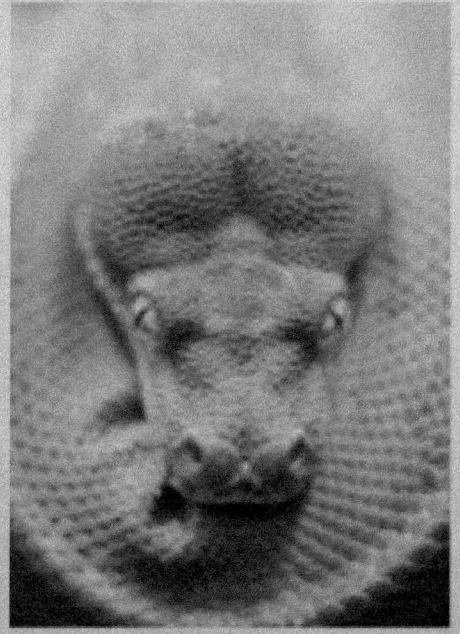

Myth: Snakes remember you if you hurt them.

Fact: Snakes are not vengeful animals and do not have the necessary intelligence to remember people or places for getting revenge. Hindi Movies (Bollywood) have a lot to do with the creation of this myth.

Myth: If one Snake is killed its partner will trace you (no matter wherever you are).

Myth: If one Snake is killed its partner will trace you (no matter wherever you are).

Fact: Snakes are not vengeful animals and are not interested in chasing or tracing people who hurt them. They do not have the necessary memory and intellect to remember people to trace them back. Neither do snakes have a feeling of camaraderie nor do snakes pair for life. Once again Bollywood is responsible for this myth.

Myth: Flying Snakes can pierce somebody's forehead or put out their eyes.

Fact: A Flying Snake does not actually fly but only glides through the air by extending its ribs and pulling in the underside. It can glide a distance of 330 feet or 100 metre.
It has an elongated head, which gives the scary feeling that it can pierce a person's head or eyes.

Myth: Snakes found in India can spit venom.

Fact: No Snake found in India can spit venom. Only Spitting-Cobras can spit venom and they are not found in India.

Myth: There are "Two-headed" snakes.

Fact: The Snake-charmers spread the myth about the Two-headed Snakes only to maintain the mythological status of the snakes in India so they can continue attracting large crowds to their Snake shows. In reality nothing like a Two-headed Snake exists.

Human beings have been afraid and fascinated by snakes since humans and snakes have been around.

Below you will find some of these mythical stories backed up by facts so that you will be able to learn the truth about snakes for yourself.

There are still many secrets about snakes that have been uncovered and if you are still fascinated about these curious creatures, you can take take it from here and get into a deeper discovery phase. Reading more books about snakes and watching some documentaries as well as diving deeper into the subjects of snakes online will help you uncover many more secrets about snakes.

You can get started with the resources section where you will find some very interesting sites online from where you can continue your journey.

If you are interest to gig a little bit deeper and learn more about snakes, please refer to the chapter "Resources".

How Bad Are Snakes Endangered Globally?

Kevin Stohlgren—Northern Scarlet Snake

Now that you hopefully can appreciate us snakes and our various species, you might be interested in some more serious stuff that concerns our future and your future at the same time because we all live on the same planet and we need to make sure that we support each other!

Did you know that some of our snakes species are declining and even endangered at the hand of humans?

Yes, it is true and we are very sad about it because we snakes have come such a long way.

Sadly, the fact is that we snakes and other endangered animals face many dangers as we are living around the world today. These are artificial dangers created by human greed and power.

Source: Dawson—Prairie Kingsnake

Declines in our reptile populations are already happening. This decline of us snake species includes mass localized extinctions and population crashes that have been noted from locations all over the globe.

Some of our snake species declines are perceived as one of the most critical threats to global biodiversity.

Our snake populations have declined significantly.

Sadly enough, we snakes are valued as food and fashion items by human beings and are thretened by these human predators on a constant basis.

We snakes have been known to survive and adapt throughout evolution and we are creatures that are well-adapted to nature and our habitats, but we are not able to adapt to artificial human activities that harm us snakes.

In nature, we snakes are facing a constant host of life and death obstacles. We are fighting a daily survival struggle against our predators.

As if that wasn't bad enough, we snakes even have to watch out for other hungry snakes because there are some snake species that eat other snakes.

Because there are so many bad guys to watch out for, we snakes have come up with a large variety of forms of protection.

To understand what really threatens the survival of our population, you must look at the harmful actions of humans and what humans do to our beautiful natural habitats.

These are the things that harm us most:

As we snakes and other reptiles are now being hunted for different purposes by human beings, even the most dangerous poisonous animals like some of us snake species have now become extinct. This type of degenerative human snake hunting behavior has caused a lot of negative impact on our environment which is why support groups have been developed over the years and today some of these organizations are pretty powerful. These organizations are helping with wildlife conservation.

There are many ways available to people to save us animals. Even the rarest animals including some of our rare snake species can be saved if people change their perspective and mindset. Knowing things and facts about endangered species like us snakes will be the first step to a better future for us snakes.

Here is what you have to consider about snake extinction.

Habitat Loss

The python's jungle habitat, for example, is disappearing. Trees are cut down for firewood and lumber. Humans are able to settle to new places and agriculture happens now where woods and forest habitats existed before.

Overexploitation

Humans have killed pythons and other snakes out of fear. All of our species have been hunted down by humans for food, for our beautiful skin, and our blood is believed to have medicinal value.

Some of our live snake buddies are even killed in Thai food markets. Our fresh blood is then drunk because people think that it helps them with their vitality. Pythons and other of us snake species are made into fashionable items like purse accessories, shoes, jackets, clothing, and belts.

We snakes are often skinned alive so as not to mark and scratch the skin and reduce our skin's commercial value. Did you know that even before snakeskin boots were trendy, our pythons buddies were considered a trophy species. They were even heavily hunted by Europeans. More recently, some of us non vemous snake species have also become sought after for pet trade and for entertainment purposes like zoos and snake charmers.

While these human acts are cruel and disasterous to our species survival, there have been developing some good people who are standing up for us and who have been helping to protect us over the past few years.

Here are the most important pro snake actions.

Conservation Actions

Trade Regulation

Our buddies the Pythons are listed in the CITES Appendix I and all trade in live python snakes or python skin products is not allowed. Poaching is considered a threat. Sadly enough illegal trade still continues.

Habitat Protection

India has established a few large areas to protect our snake habitats. These snake reserves are unpopular with people who live close because they are afraid to go into the forests to get firewood. Rampant poaching is still a problem and has been addressed. In fact, in some places armed-guard patrols have to make sure that poaching does not take place.

A better solution would be to give those people a controlled access and a better education about how conservation is helping people and animals in a concerted effort. People need to learn in which way both human beings and wildlife can co-exist.

Indian Wildlife (Protection) Act 1972

Did you know that the Irulas tribe of Andhra Pradesh and Tamil Nadu in India have been snake hunters and gatherers in India?

They have been able to develop their talent in the dry and hot plains forests. They have practiced the art of catching a snake from generation to generation. These Indian hunters have a vast knowledge in the field of snakes. THe Irulus tribe is generally catching the snakes with the help of a simple wooden stick. Before the ban, these hunters have caught loads of snakes and sold them to the snake skin industries worldwide.

However, after the complete snake catching ban in India and the Indian Wildlife (Protection) Act 1972, these snake hunters formed the Irula Snake Catcher's Cooperative. They also switched to catching snakes for removal of their venom. Once they removed the venom they set the snakes free again and release them in the wild.

This venom is very valuable because it is used for producing life-saving medicinal products and for research.

These Irulas tribes are also known to consume the snake meat. Others have found a very effective application by using it as rat extermination in villages.

Snake charmers, snake catchers, and snake wranglers all a threat to us.

Snake trapping like it has been developed as a trend does involve a herpetologist. Snake trappers are using a long V-shaped stick while others prefer to us their bare hands.

All these snake involving activities are considered cruel and therefore people who were concerened with this issue have been developing organizations in order to help protect animal rights.

The Wildlife Protection Act of 1972 in India, for example, is a law that is technically proscribing snake charming and snake charmers on grounds of reducing animal cruelty.

There are other environment laws that are proscribing thes snake charming practices and thus this activity becomes less and less popular in today's society.

These animal rights are there because some awesome, caring, and responsible human beings were able to identify and fight for our cause.

However we need more initiative for our cause because our extinction would be a natural disaster because we are all dependent on each other - humans and animals are dependent on each other in order to keep a good balance of the ecosystem and this is what is called interdependence.

Lastly, you should know that in general we are peaceful animals if we are not attacked.

However, some of us have learned over the centuries how to protect themselves from predators by the means of poisonous venom, but there are others of us snakes that are peaceful animals and these snakes rather hide or run.

We are not looking to attack or pick an aggressive fight with humans unless they attack and try to grab and grope us!

We also add our natural beauty to the earth, the forests, and the water.

There is one difference though, we do not kill humans unless they attack and try to kill us first

There is one thing that you must absolutely remember about us snakes. We can be sneaky and we do have a 6th sense.

We are also smart and wise because otherwise we would not have been able to survive for millions of years until today so please do respect us for who we are and if you have the appropriate knowledge about us you will know that unless we are attacked or threatened (unintentionally and intentinally), we will not attack you first!

We have survived until today because we were smart and wise enough to adapt through evolution. Evolution has taught us how to protect ourselves from predators over the years and this is why we are looked upon as dangerous and dark by people who don't know us!

As you have learned by now some of our snake species are pretty poisonous towards any predator who tries to cross us!

However, not all of us are as strong and poisonous as the venomous snakes so that life becomes a daily threatful experience for most of us.

This is why we need your help in order to survive. Humans can protect us and give us a safe environment were we can live in a happy and balanced self sustained life.

In captivity, many of us snake species can live for surprisingly very long times. The average of American snakes is somewhere between 18 and 20 years in captivity. One snake that was captivated in the Philadelphia Zoo broke a record because the snake lived up to an age of 46 years.

If you have not read the previous chapter yet, please make sure to read it because this will help you understand why we are truly awesome and amazing creatures and why you must absolutely help us survive!

Please refer to the next chapter "Please Help Us" where you can see how your initiative might save our species!

Please Help Us

We snakes do live a longer lifespan if we live in a protected environment like a zoo or a protected home. As you learned in the chapter before, one of us snakes even reached the age of 46 in a captivated zoo environment!

In general we are a non threatening species if we are not attacked first. Otherwise some of us can turn into pretty poisonous creatures to defend themselves.

To protect us some responsible human beings have developed protection programs for us so that we can live a peaceful life in harmony.

However, if we snakes live in the wild, we do fear humans who are ignorant of our space and natural habitats.

Today, more and more of us snakes are captivated in zoos around the globe and we are taken care of via some cool humans and their protection programs. Thes humans show initiative for our case.

It is very sad that we need such protection programs as opposed to being able to survive ourselves in the wild nature like the rules of mother nature are suggesting it.

However, we are not capable to follow mother nature's law because of some ignorant human beings who harm and kill us and we are therefore very thankful for these protected places that have been created for us and for our survival.

Some humans do a lot to help us and to make sure that we snakes are well taken care of.

Thanks to all of those people who are actively helping us through their initiatives.

On the other side, there are other humans who can truly be a serious threat to us snakes.

We fear humans who do not respect our freedom and rights. We fear the people who keep hunting us because they think we taste good or look good as a fashion accessory.

We fear the people who hunt us down for their own benefits and profit.

The best way to help us snakes is to refuse buying and consuming snake skin products and by showing some inititative for our cause.

Conservation efforts and breeding programs are in place to restore our population to a normal level.

Today there are animal rights and laws in place that makes hunting for us and destructing our habitats an illegal act.

Thanks for your engagement and initiative in putting out this message to everyone you know because you can make a huge difference! If everybody will put out the message like you do, our terrible endangered condition that we live in today might change for the better tomorrow!

We love peace, we are generally peaceful animals if we are not attacked and hunted down by cruel humans, and we enjoy our freedom and happiness.

If you love us snakes, too, make sure to defend us against these animal haters who do not seem to care about us and who hunt us down for their own benfits and money gains.

Thanks for sharing the message and thanks for being our fan and friend!

...and make sure to put out this message to others because we are an endangered species and we need Your HELP!

Everybody around the planet needs to get this message!

Bonus: Can Humans Eat Snakes?

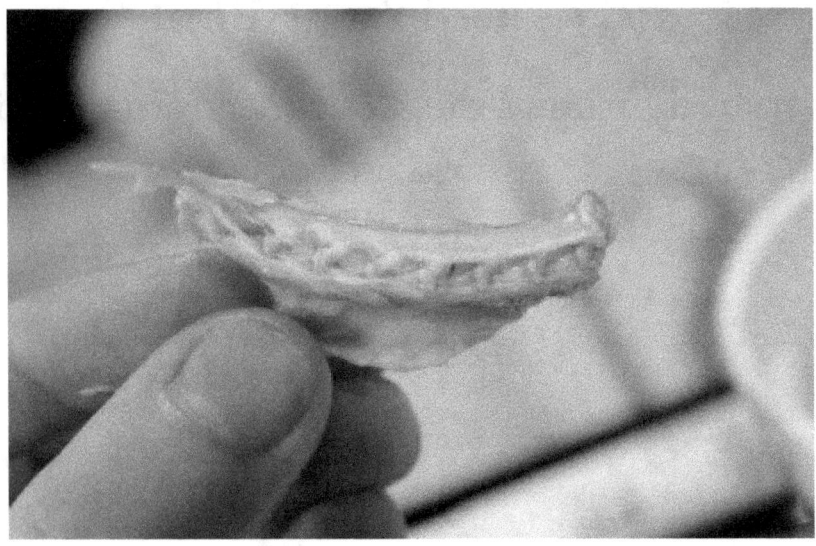

Source: Max P Vanderheyden—Snake Meat in Taipei

The venom in a snake is in its glands in its head. People who like to eat snake meat cut off the head and prepare the meat in various styles.

Fried rattlesnake meat, for example, is a delicacy in Arizona or New Mexico.

The snake meat is considered a delicacy in most places. In reality, however, this fact is true likely more to its rarity rather than delicious taste!

Most snake meat is stringy, light colored, and fairly chewy.

It is very low in fat and easy to digest.

Some cultures hold it in very high regard as a healing, healthy, energy-enhancing food.

In any case, it is entirely edible and, properly prepared, very tasty.

The concern over poison being in the meat should be relieved by the fact that all venom is in the jaw area removed with the head.

If the snake has struck itself or been bitten by another snake, it is comforting to note that cooking removes all risks!

Actually, the venom of most snakes can be ingested even fresh with no ill effect! Just eat and enjoy without worry.

The meat is going to taste much like how it is fixed, seasoned, and cooked.

Prepared like fish with corn meal, it will remind you of fish.

Prepared like chicken, with a flour dip, it will taste strikingly like chicken.

It can be smoked, broiled, boned for gumbo, made into pate, and basically cooked any way that is the favorite of the cook.

Whether you've bought fresh snake meat at a market where snake meat is a popular food item or you got it some place else, snake meat tasts between fish and chicken. It is between fish and chicken in flavor and in texture.

It can be prepard to look like either a chicken or a fish dish.

Did you love *Snake Discovery Kids: Jungle Stories Of Mysterious & Dangerous Snakes With Funny Pictures, Photos & Memes Of Snakes For Children*? Then you should read *Frogs And Toads Discovery: Frog Picture Book For Kids With Fun Photos & Illustrations* by Kate Cruso!

Does your child love frogs and toads? Inside Frogs And Toads Discovery: Frog Picture Book For Kids With Fun Photos &Illustrations your child will discover:* Frog Pictures * Frogs & Toads Differences* Frogs Around The World?* Funny Frog Stories * Amazing Frog Facts For Kids * Most Poisonous Frogs On Earth* The Weirdest Looking Toads & Frogs* Most Bizarre Frogs On Earth* Weirdest Frogs On Earth* Interesting, Curious & Intriguing Facts About Frogsmore... This book will take your child through a journey of fun facts, amazing discoveries, curious and intriguing stories about frogs.You will find some interesting revelations and secrets you probably never heard about frogs.Some myths and truths, and other curious stuff about frogs that children just find cool and groovy to know are also included.This book will take your child through a journey of fun facts, amazing discoveries, curious and intriguing stories about frogs, and hilarious pictures about frogs.You will find some interesting revelations & secrets you probably never heard about.Some myths and truths, and other curious stuff about frogs that children just find cool and groovy to know are also included.For example, did you know that there is a type of poison dart frog that is called the blue jeans frog?In captivity, many of us frog species and toads, can live for surprisingly very long times. The average is somewhere between four and fifteen years!and more... This is a book series inspired by kids for kids!Kids learn about new and interesting facts so that a combination of both the curious and the new materials and facts together with the visual aspect of the pictures.Children are entertained with the coolness factor of the discovery book plus they learn some new and a little bit harder to retain facts simultaneously with the cool stuff and this is how the child is going to retain all of the information. The discovery books work in synchronization with the brain and not against the brain like some dull textbooks try to teach things.It is a fact that kids just love these discovery picture books about weird animals and weird stuff that the animals are doing because they love the coolness and grooviness factor of the books. Parents are super satisfied because their children show interest for things on a higher level of interest as usual. The discovery concept of this frog book for example transforms a little bit more dry information and facts into brain friendly information that the child will retain & that the child will be able to use as active information later on.This discover book is brain friendly and works in synchronization with your child's brain not against it. If your child asks lots of questions you actually have the proof that providing discovery books to your child actually works because children who discover with their own senses and in an active and interactive way are able to develop intelligence on a much higher level than children who are not asking any questions and who are passively sitting in front of a TV all day long. Stimulation of thought and contemplation increases intelligence and the brain power and TV kills the brain cells of your child.Parents & home-schoolers alike are reporting unprecedented results from using her books as learning materials & they get results even with children who usually hate reading books & have to learn dry information.

Also by Kate Cruso

Discovery Books For Kids Series
Frogs And Toads Discovery: Frog Picture Book For Kids With Fun Photos & Illustrations
Panda Discovery Kids: Jungle Stories of Cute Panda Bears with Funny Pictures, Photos & Memes of Pandas for Children
Seaturtle Discovery Kids: Sea Stories Of Cute Sea Turtles With Funny Pictures, Photos & Memes Of Seaturtles For Children

Standalone
Snake Discovery Kids: Jungle Stories Of Mysterious & Dangerous Snakes With Funny Pictures, Photos & Memes Of Snakes For Children

About the Publisher

InfinitYou is a hybrid general interest trade publisher. One of the first of its kind InfinitYou publishes physical books, electronic books, and audiobooks in various genres. Our publications are meant to educate, edify and entertain readers of all walks of life from babies to the elderly. Home to more than twenty imprints such as Infinit Baby, Infinit Kids, Infinit Girl, Infinit Boy, Infinit Coloring, Infinit Swear Words, Infinit Activities, Infinit Productivity, Infinit Cat, Infinit Dog, Infinit Love, Infinit Family, Infinit Survival, Infinit Health, Infinit Beauty, Infinit Spirituality, Infinit Lifestyle, Infinit Wealth, Infinit Romance, and lots more.